THE MEANING
OF CHRISTMAS

Edited by

Sarah Marshall

First published in Great Britain in 2005 by
ANCHOR BOOKS
Remus House,
Coltsfoot Drive,
Peterborough, PE2 9JX
Telephone (01733) 898102

All Rights Reserved

Copyright Contributors 2005

SB ISBN 1 84418 394 7

FOREWORD

Anchor Books is a small press, established in 1992, with the aim of promoting readable poetry to as wide an audience as possible.

We hope to establish an outlet for writers of poetry who may have struggled to see their work in print.

The poems presented here have been selected from many entries, and as always editing proved to be a difficult task.

I trust this selection will delight and please the authors and all those who enjoy reading poetry.

Sarah Marshall
Editor

CONTENTS

Christmas	Nadine Mackie	1
It's Getting Close to Christmas Down On Christmas Street	Stephen A Owen	2
It's Christmas Time	Christine Lemon	4
Don't Call On Me Saint Nicholas	Michael James Treacy	5
Packing Away Christmas	Carol Ann Darling	6
Daddy Will Be Here Soon	Cardinal Cox	7
Christmas 2004	Doris E Pullen	8
A Special Time - Christmas Eve	George Carrick	9
Christmas Day	Richard Mahoney	9
Christmas By Far!	Tony Pratt	10
Christmas Is Coming	Lisa Platts	12
Christmas Eve	Eddie Jepson	13
Christmas	Pamela Popp	14
Festive Season	Lisa Anne Oram	14
Christmas Meaning	Sue Ireland	15
Christmas	Amy Clift	16
Christmas Joy	Ruth Fellows	17
A Christmas Revelation 2004	Lorna Tippett	18
The Meaning Of Christmas	Diana Lynch	19
Christmas Of Goodwill	Michael D Bedford	19
The Christmas Lottery	Frances Roberts	20
Arboreal Santa	Megan Davies	20
A Homeless Christmas - From Me	Karen Ferrari	21
Bloomin' Christmas	Steve Cannon	22
Thank You Mama	Nyasha John Musimwa	23
A Saviour's Birth	Bob Pierce	24
Christmas 2004	Barbara Balmer	24
Santa's Christmas	Patricia Whorwood	25
Christmas Love And Light	Gordon Forbes	26
Christmas Eve	A F Mace	27
Another Christmas Time	David Woods	27
The Night That Santa Comes	Mark Jacobs	28
Christmas 2001	Marian Clark	30
Christmas	Bill Surman	31

Noel Au Pai's #8221 (Christmas In The Homeland)	Gladys Bruno	32
Messiah	Brian Henry	33
Skipping Christmas	Muriel Nicola Waldt	34
Christmas	Ceri Siân	35
Christmas Wish	Victoria Morley	36
Christmas	Barbara M Beatson	37
Christmas	Simone C Summerscales	38
Christmas	Dorothy Neil	39
Star Children	D M Neu	40
An Angel Of The Lord	Olliver Charles	41
What Is Christmas?	Ken Copley	42
Christmas Cards	Colin Shaw	43
Christmas Tree	Theresa M Carrier	43
The Old Grey Ball	C Umpleby	44
A Christmas Message	Allen Jessop	45
Christmas	Pat Jakes	45
A Special Christmas Visitor	Margaret M Donnelly	46
The Christmas Snowman	Linda Francis	47
My Thingamajig	Terry J Powell	48
Same Day, Different Year	Karen Roberts	48
Baubles	Kathy Rawstron	49
Christmas Cheer	H G Booley	49
Christmas Shopping	Jackie Johnson	50
Christmas Poem	Sarah Heptinstall	50
Song For The Children	Grace Divine	51
Mother And Baby, Fine	Richard Stead	51
Christmas Words . . . Whilst Shopping	Jessie Morton	52
Untitled	Jay Berkowitz	52
Something Special At Christmas	Hannah Ryan	53
Jingle All The Way	Joanna Lloyd-Barrett	53
Christmas Time	A F Hiscocks	54
Poem To Santa	Katie Richards	54
What Is Christmas?	Margaret B Baguley	55
Christmas	Colin Zarhett	55
Christmas	Franz	56
Christmas	Joyce Smith	57

Christmas Celebration	Joan Earle Broad	58
Happy Holy Days	Mary Cathleen Brown	58
Untitled	S Pritchard	59
Homecoming	Carolyn Smith	59
The Patience Of God	Geoffrey T Perry	60
Baby	Irene Clare Garner	60
Like Gentle Snow	Richard J Bradshaw	61
Earth's Angels	Brian Tallowin	61
Christmas Is Nothing	Emma Akuffo	62
A Saviour Is Born	Susan Byers	62
Snow	Jasmina Trifunovic	63
Gift Of Gifts	Kirk Antony Watson	63
Christmas	Evelyn Westwood	64
The Real Christmas	Benjamin McCanna	64
Christmas Though The Eyes Of A Child	Sophia Cartland	65
Lonely At Christmas	Bav	65
Fidleye Fee, Fidleye Foe	Simon Knight	66
A Christmas Feeling	Natasha Palmer	66
Christmas Wishes	Marion McGarrigle	67
The Round Robin Letter	Marion Scourfield	67
Happy Christmas	Pam Eaves	68
December Dawn	Peter Morriss	68
The Spirit Of Christmas	Keith Beasley	69
A Christmas Poem	Peter Woolley	69
Christmas	Julliet Miller	70
Giving	Philip Housbey	70
Christmas	Irene Greenan	71
Midnight Communion	Idris Woodfield	71
A Reason For Christmas	John Morris	72
Christmas	Michelle Borrett	73
The Child Of The Manger - Yet A King	Frances M Gorton	74
It Comes Every Year	Michael Hutchinson	75
When Camels Blinked	C C	76
Christmas Journey	Olive Bedford	77
The Lord's Birthday	June Davies	78

I've Seen Santa Claus!	Paul Wilkins	78
Christmas - Without Christ?	Nita Roskilly	79
Our Christmas Sonnet 2004	Mary May Robertson	79
A Quiet True Christmas	Adegoke Austin Adedamola	80
Star Of Bethlehem	Barbara Holme	81
Christmas Joy	Mary Frances Mooney	82
Christmas Approaches Like A Wave	Susan Wren	82
The Essence Of Christmas	Opal Innsbruk	83
Christmas (Credit) Cards	Stein Dunne	83
Christmas	Brin Parsons	84
Christmas Wish	Anita Layland	84
Before Christmas Should Leave Us	Don Harris	85
The Secret Christmas Present	Camille Gillon	85
A Winter's Imprint	Darryl Benson	86
Deep Meaning	Shirley Parker	86
Crackers About Christmas	Penny Miller	87
The Christmas I Forgot	Ann Wood	87
Phenomenon	Lorna Lea	88
The Star	Pauline Phillips	89
Prayer For Christmas - The Gift Of Hope	Maria Dabrowska	90
Christmas In The Desert	Winifred Curran	90
Danni's Christmas	Danni Render	91
Christmas	J Sayner	91
The Greatest Gift	Tola Ajala	92
Christmas Came Early	Ian Duncan	92
Nearly Twenty-Five	Michael Gavin	93
Snowflakes	Eliza Hickinson	93
Christmas Sonnet	Judith Hinds	94
The Flippant Housewife	Beryl Messham	94
A Christmas Wish	Vera Parsonage	95
The Glory Of Christmas	Patricia Cruzan	96
Christmas Tree	Karen Giles	97
The Invisible Love	Frank L Appleyard	98
Madonna And Child	Bob White	99
Winter Picture	Beverley Morton	100

A Jolly Holly Christmas	Maureen Reynolds	101
Come To Bethlehem	Patricia Adele Draper	102
Getting Ready For Christmas	Rosemary Davies	103
Little Infant's Time	Joyan Jomond	104
Christmas Present Bus Stop	Daniel Brendan Courtney	105
Christmas Laughter	Norma Griffiths	106
What Is Christmas?	Joan Williams	107
Bethlehem	D A Sheasby	108
Christmas Whispers	Paul Barrington	109
Take A Break	Barbara Dunning	110
Christmas Can Be Lonely	Denise Castellani	111
Thoughts Of Christmas	Gail Wooton	112
A Christmas Thought	Thelma Cook	113
Winter Warms The Soul Within Me	Joyce Hemsley	114
Festive Spirits	Don Capo	115
That Christmas Gift	Erica Menzies	116
Christmas Eve	Emma Kay	117
New Year	Sarah-Jane Clark	118
Happy Christmas	Margaret Mansbridge	119
Celebrating Christmas	Anne Gray	120
Cold Christmas	Jane Margaret Isaac	121
Christmas Eve	Shanu Goyal	122
Christmas Loneliness	J J Saunders	123
Christmas Is Here	Callum Smith	124
St Peter's Church, On Boxing Day Morning	Rodger Moir	125
Christmas True	BMF	126
Christmas	Rose Ashwell	127
Cat Christmas	Moira Jean Clelland	128
Jingle Boll*x	Paul Andrews	129
Peace On Earth	Rebecca Walker	130
Christmas Time	Joyce Hallifield	131
A Christmas Thought	Lynne Cassels	132
Presents For Others	Jennifer Davey	133
A Fall Of Snow	Mike Harrison	134
Christmas Alone	Carol Paxton	135
Alone At Christmas	Mary Howcroft	136

Reminiscence	Muriel Bransdon	137
Oh Christmas	Emma Jo Taranaski	138
How Much For Christmas Day	Francis McGarry	139
Christmas Day	Jacky Griffiths	140
Christmas Time	Barry Ryan	141
Christmas 2004	H A J Fletcher	142
Christmas Day	Walter Dalton	143
Christmas Is Forever	Vincent Malawo	144
A Christmas Dilemma	F G Ward	145
They Believe Again!	Laraine Smith	146
Christmas Tree	Anne-Marie Lloyd-Barrett	147
A Christmas Parable	Rita Hardiman	148
Starlight	Marjorie Lloyd	149
Father Christmas	Angela Kilvert-King	150
I Remember The Reason	Nigel Lloyd Maltby	151
A Family Christmas	Gerald Hampshire	152
The Holly	June Coral Dye	153
Mystery	Ruth Walker	154
Spare A Dime	April Dickinson-Owen	155
Food For Thought	Dorothy M Mitchell	156
Hey, Santa	Wendy Orlando & Emma Orlando	157
It's That Time Of Year	Georgie Roomes	158
A Message Of Peace	Ruth Dewhirst	159
Through A Child's Eyes	Tracey Clayton	160
Song For A Time	John Eccles	161
Red Breast	Nicky Anderson	162
The Reason For The Season	Timothy Cross	163
It's Christmas Soon	Judie Archer	164
Christmas	Jo Lewis	165
Well, It's Christmas . . . Isn't It?	Sally Drury	166
Clouded By Sadness	Jo Lees	167
Christmas	Dan Chellumben	168
Message Of Joy	Patricia Spear	169
The Christ Of Christmas	Derek Sones	170
Joyeux Noel	Joseph Larkin	171
Christmas Shopping	Gill D'Arcy	172
The Snowflake Catcher	Gail Anselmi	173

At Christmas	Margery Rayson	174
Christmas Is Bliss	Susan E Powell	175
Christmas Fairy	Pandy Pond	176
White Christmas	Margaret Blight	177
Christmas Day	Christine Shelley	178
I'd Love To Be An Angel	Alison Gorton	179
Oh Where Did Christmas Go?	John Simpson	180
Santa Magic	Elizabeth Hiddleston	181
A Modern Christmas Carol	Terry Ireland	182
Giving To Receive	Hugh Ortega Breton	183
Santa's Visit	H Lamb	184
Christmas 2005	Joan Peacock	185
Christmas Sleighing	Mark Guy	186
Poem For Christmas	Janet Hopkins	187
Can't Wait For Christmas	Jennifer Oxley	188
Angels Carolling Hymns	Elizabeth Bowes	189
Christmas	Jack Scrafton	190
Revelation	Michael Fenton	191
Christmas On The Beach	Tamsin Quantrell	192
Solitary Star	Elizabeth C Millar	193
Starlight Express	Beryl Moorehead	194
Jingle All The Way	Ian W Wilkinson	195
At Last I Knew	Tom Roach	196
Christmas Angel	Norman Bissett	197
The Double Tastes Of Christmas Time	Justice N Okafor	198
The Christmas Masquerade	Tommy McBride	199
'For Unto Us A Child Is Born'	Gerasim	200
Waiting For Santa	Mary Lawson	201
Santa's Adventurous Journey	Jean P McGovern	202
Home For Christmas	Lesley Britton	203
Christmas Essentials	Freda Grieve	204
Christmas Shopping Blues	Peter G H Payne	205
Christmas	Martha Ann D'Souza	206
Looking Forward To Next Christmas	Anne Rainbow	207
Christmas Catastrophe	Pat Heppel	208

CHRISTMAS

Remember it's a time for giving,
Renewed dreams and praises for Jesus.
Let us be wiseman bearing gifts.
Beautiful lights and candles are like stars in the night.
Sparkling décor for the little tree and loads of presents too.
But a white Christmas is on everyone's wish list,
Snowmen everywhere will jump off the old mantle,
When that first winter snow falls.
Time to get the woollies,
And build snowmen outdoors.
Remember the little snowman?
Blowing smoke when he shouldn't,
Grandad's pipe suited Sherlock Holmes better.
A little smoke soon came to rest.
Christmas! is a time for peace?
Time for all the old rumours to turn to ice,
Melting away as each candle is lit.
Bringing prayers and hope to a nation.
So give someone a candle this Christmas,
A snowman if you wish.
Christmas! The little note should read,
I might be seasonal but I will be back again,
With a whole new start to life.
So light this little candle every night for the season,
Bringing light and joy into my soul,
Leaving me as a little star to guide others to a better life.
Remembering in my witness, peace for all,
Portraying God's love is for all.
Christmas!

Nadine Mackie

IT'S GETTING CLOSE TO CHRISTMAS DOWN ON CHRISTMAS STREET

(Got this idea from the Liverpool and Everton derby game, just thought I'd change a few names, make it more comical)

It's getting close to Christmas down on Christmas Street
The elves are having a football game
It's their annual meet
With one player short in goal
Santa has been called in
He's a merry old soul
He won't let many in
He used to be Lapland's number one
Now the new kid on the block is his youngest born son
Stevie Claus is a striker and captains Liverudolf FC
With a bunch of elves from Santa's academy
The game's a 3 o'clock kick off
On the field next to the weeping willow tree
The ref blows the whistle
When the big finger hits three

With two minutes gone Santa's team are already one up
Thanks to Milan Elos
Chipped the ball over the stranded elf in the green jersey top
But he got booked for throwing his shirt to the crowd
Hit Mother Claus in the face
She screamed for joy out loud
Didi Elfman
Made it number two
Harry Elf hit the third and shouted thank you
But the best was still to come in the second half
Thanks to their new signing Santa's youngest son
He picked up the ball just inside his own half

Passed to Louis Elfia
One two with a little tease
Beat a few more players
With the greatest of ease

Cut inside left
Brushed past the ref
Let go from outside the box
Ref took his pen and notepad out from his socks
In the top left hand corner
The goalkeeper took a deep breath
Dived to the right
Ball swerved left
Power took it into the net
Stevie celebrated pointing his finger
As he took the ball from the net

Full time it was five-two
Santa's team got a penalty
Very late on as they always do
The other team got awarded a dodgy own goal
Poor old Santa had fallen asleep in his goal
By the time he was woken it was too late
You could have heard a pin drop
The look on the old geezer's face
He took down the opposing elf
Stamped on both of his feet
The poor elf fell to the floor
He was as white as a sheet

After the match the winners received their wine
Two days to Christmas they had plenty of time
If you get a football for Christmas make sure it's brand new
Cos I remember seeing Santa
Taking a sponge and bucket of hot water into the loo
So to next year let's see what the Elves can do
Right now they are like the Toffees
Getting beaten five-two.

Stephen A Owen

IT'S CHRISTMAS TIME

Dance for joy! It's Christmas time!
Please come and make a ring.
Join hands around the tree so bright;
As the music starts let's sing.
    We'll sing a song about the tree
    Which stands in splendour now;
    Swathed with glittering tinsel,
    Baubles hung on every bough.
Every bough is evergreen
And fills the room with scent.
The sweet perfume pervades the air -
Do you know what's meant?
    It means that Jesus Christ is born,
    His love extends to all.
    And we His people here on Earth
    Must answer to His call.
He calls us now at Christmas time
To remember Bethlehem,
Where He was born so long ago
To die and live again.
    The tree's alive, it's evergreen
    To show eternity.
    We move around to left and right
    Dancing round the tree.
Dance for joy! It's Christmas time!
Do come and make a ring.
Give your thanks to Jesus Christ
Who gave us everything.

Christine Lemon

DON'T CALL ON ME SAINT NICHOLAS

Cold winds blow through city streets
as winter's grip takes hold
and downbeat folk in downbeat worlds
retreat to lives untold.

Rain lashed pavements now are bare,
there's little chance of snow,
but in a bleak, northern climate
an oasis starts to glow.

Christmas days are here again,
those warm, enchanting times.
A chance to cast off gloomy dawns,
relive those joyful climes.

Don't call on me, Saint Nicholas -
just pass me by this year.
Life's been good to me once more,
no cause to shed a tear.

Haunted people turn in angst -
no light in vacant stares.
Spend your time with such as these
and show them someone cares.

Winter's chill now stalks the land,
those dark, foreboding clouds
but Christmas cheer brings happiness
to man's enduring crowds.

Please call on me, Saint Nicholas,
next year at Christmas time -
I may be a grey-faced one
in need of love, sublime.

Michael James Treacy

PACKING AWAY CHRISTMAS

I'm dreaming of a . . .

You get them out,
You put them up,
You take them down,
You put them away,
That's what Christmas decorations are all about.

And before you know it,
You get them out,
You put them up,
You take them down,
And it's another Christmas,
But will it snow a bit?

Packing away Christmas,
Undressing the tree,
Removing all the sparkling silver and grand golden balls,
Ritually, carefully.
Of unwinding the tinsel,
I'm not very fond,
Gone the fragile fairy on the top,
With the magical wizzy wand.

You get them out,
You put them up,
You take them down,
That's what Christmas decorations are all about.

But what if we left them up all year?

No way, I hear you shout.
So, you get them out,
You put them up,
You take them down,
That's what Christmas decorations are all about.

All the shining stars,
All the shimmering snowflakes,
Being packed away,
Gives my heart a little ache.
All the cotton wool stuffed snowmen,
And the Father Christmas hat,
Tucked away safely,
With the festive this and that.

And before you know it,
You get them out,
You put them up,
You take them down,
That's what Christmas decorations are all about.

And I'm dreaming of a . . .

Carol Ann Darling

DADDY WILL BE HERE SOON

Tree half bald, fairy askew
Needles trampled in till May
No snow in the garden
Neighbour's kid pedals first bike
Bell ringing, screams of skinned knees
Presents lie waiting - not opened
On television there's a children's hospital
She's sweating over food that
Would fill them all day
Even as the Queen starts to speak
There are no tyres stopping outside
    The phone rings
    No one wants to answer.

Cardinal Cox

CHRISTMAS 2004

Another year gone and I'm eighty-three,
My eyes are dimmer but I can still see.
I have hair on my head, and wobbly teeth
But I can still open my mouth and speak.

It's Christmas again, and my family are here.
We've had Christmas dinner and plenty of cheer -
Some special fizzy drink and whisky galore
And the Christmas pudding went down well as of yore.

How glad I am that the Christmas chores
Do still come along, which makes life less of a bore.
I've been lucky so long, and think I'm very blessed
To have friends who all help me, and love you can test.

My angels look after me and give me help
When I get into trouble and feel I could yelp.
But my friends stand by me, these I can see
They are gathered around with my family.

So to all of you now I will raise my glass,
Say, 'To Hell with the Devil and a kick up the bottom.'
Forget the past - just live for the present,
It's all we've got until we get to Heaven!

Doris E Pullen

A Special Time - Christmas Eve

The expectation, all the preparations, coming to an end.
Last minute shopping nearly over, no more cards to write or send.
The buzz, that lovely feeling, you know tomorrow will bring,
The family around you, celebration, tinsel, tree, joyous carols to sing.
Presents, all wrapped, stockings hung, Santa ready, and on his way,
Ever busy hands, from eager helpers, Rudolf and Co
                                        waiting at the sleigh.
Table set, crackers at the ready, the turkey prepared for tomorrow,
Thinking, wouldn't it be lovely, if we had a covering of snow.
Little ones in bed, all clean and shiny, eyes sparkling, trying to sleep,
Your thoughts of past loved ones, in your heart they lie so deep.
Settling down together, a deserved tot, a relaxing nightcap shared,
A last look, just before midnight, all the presents now
                                        down from upstairs.
A glass of wine and cake for the welcome guest,
                                      to show that you believe,
I love Christmas Day, but for me, it's such a special time,
                                          on Christmas Eve.

George Carrick

Christmas Day

On this day may we enjoy the peace
That others haven't got.
We send them greetings wherever they may be.
A simple thought could mean so much.
Let the hand of friendship reach out with a gentle
Touch and bring them comfort
On this Christmas Day.

Richard Mahoney

CHRISTMAS BY FAR!

Christmas candles burning bright,
   Shiny star glowing white,
Deep within clear moonlit sky,
   Children question and wonder why?
Then as they sleep in peaceful rest,
   Dreams of St Nicholas come to test.

Choirs of angels sing outside,
   Sounds of hooves . . . open sleigh ride,
Then as the soft white snow does fall,
   Harmony settles for one and all,
A year of hardship draws to an end,
   As enemies reconcile their troubled friends.

Bethlehem, a donkey, a cold winter's night,
   Angels and shepherds - startled with fright,
A bright shining star, way up high,
   Shows the way for three kings in the cold night sky,
Purple haze and golden morn,
   Today's the day 'a child is born'.

Bringing kin and kind together,
   Travelling from far, in the bleakest weather,
Shared special moments as girls and boys return home,
   Parents comforted, no longer alone,
Then memories of those who we still hold dear,
   Are with us forever as we end the year!

Food aplenty, and glasses chilled,
   Children's pleasure as stockings are filled,
As smiles and laughter fill the air,
   They act the fool without a care,
A special touch in a special way,
   To make this a magical Christmas Day!

Then the crackers are pulled and the fights begin,
    Children squealing and making a din,
Is the turkey cooked or is it over-done,
    Will there be enough for everyone?
Christmas pudding with custard, and pies with cream,
    Brandy and sherry as the plates are wiped clean.

Then in front of the telly for the annual repeat,
    Whilst a walk outside offers others retreat!
A hush on the roads and still in the air,
    A silence so special, a peace so rare!
Now what about those who are a little less well,
    The homeless, the hungry, those locked in a cell?

Families working through times of stress,
    Those who have a whole lot less,
The weak, the young, the old and the poor,
    A brother, a sister or the child next-door,
Spare a thought and a little time,
    For those locked up for their crime.

For the ill and the dying or the newly bereaved,
    It's Christmas for them amongst all you've received,
Food for the homeless and food for thought,
    Is Christmas just about all that you've brought?
A simple 'hello' may be your gift,
    Or a simple 'I'm sorry!' to end that rift.

An outstretched hand or an outpoured heart,
    Is all that you need to do your part,
Enjoy your warmth and festive cheer,
    But spare a thought for others at this time of year.
Love your family and hold them close,
    But above all else remember this most,

It's great to receive sweets, chocolates and brittle,
    But more special *by far*, to give just a little!

Tony Pratt

CHRISTMAS IS COMING

I wrap my coat tighter around myself as I stroll down the street.
The snow crunching loudly beneath my feet.
Everywhere I turn I see the same sight, snow covering everything
And it's looking so bright.

Christmas is coming and it's coming so fast,
The happiness and festivities they never seem to last.
When the holiday is over we act like it never was,
Why do we forget the good times so fast?

I come across a house that looks very old.
It looks like a Christmas card, so beautiful and bold.
The winter is here, I see and feel it in the air.

Christmas is coming and it's coming so fast,
The happiness and festivities they never seem to last.
When the holiday is over we act like it never was,
Why do we forget the good times so fast?

I walk inside the old house and find myself looking around,
An open fire is blazing, looking at it makes me smile.
I am where I belong, like someone was expecting me.
I remove my coat, sit and watch the fire burning
But something is missing, why do I feel this yearning?

Christmas is coming and it's coming so fast,
The happiness and festivities they never seem to last.
When the holiday is over we act like it never was,
Why do we forget the good times so fast?

Then I turn my head as he enters the room.
This is the part of me that has been missing.
I look at him as he sits beside me
And pull him close for a Christmas kiss.

Christmas is coming and it's coming so fast,
The happiness and festivities they never seem to last.
When the holiday is over we act like it never was,
Why do we forget the good times so fast?

Lisa Platts

CHRISTMAS EVE

A light shone down from beyond the stars
Was it a sign from Heaven
Which would heal our scars
It was on Christmas Eve
When this glorious sight
Turned the darkness into light

Was it God's way of bestowing
His love for us all
By showing
A miraculous sight
On Christmas Eve night
A light that would set out hearts glowing

And on the following day
In our church we would pray
And thanks would be said
And psalms would be read
Hymns would be sung
And church bells rung

Expressing our feelings
On this special day.

Eddie Jepson

CHRISTMAS

The Christmas cards have all been sent
The presents now are ready
The fairy lights all brightly shine
And snow is falling steady
Then in the far off distance
I can see the church steeple
Ringing out the message
Telling all the people
To celebrate the birth of Christ
To join the carol singing
Forget about financial stress
Christmas to you is bringing
Go out and meet the people
The lonely and the poor
Then, put out the welcome mat
And open up your door.

Pamela Popp

FESTIVE SEASON

Winter is here,
And Christmas is very near,
A season of goodwill,
Christmas turkey and beer.
Decorating the Christmas tree,
Giving people gifts for free,
Watching all the festive films,
Eating food as though you have worms.
A new year will soon begin,
I wonder what it will bring,
After the festive season has been.

Lisa Anne Oram

CHRISTMAS MEANING

A star appears in the eastern sky
Whilst the bells on Earth do ring.
A stable echoes to a baby's cry
As a choir of angels sing.

This infant in a manger,
Whose birth was long foretold.
To a world so full of danger.
Born in an animal fold.

Shepherds kneeled before Him,
Wise men their gifts did bring.
To pay homage to the Christ child
Who one day would be king.

For God had sent Himself to us
To dwell in human form.
A babe who'd grow to light our way
And lead us through life's storm.

So remember, at this time of year
When the hullabaloo does cease,
That Jesus was born at Christmas time
To guide the world to peace.

Sue Ireland

CHRISTMAS

Peace and goodwill to all mankind,
That is what we were blessed you'll find,
Sadly that is no longer the case,
Not in this day and age for the human race.

People still suffer now all over the Earth,
Even despite the holy birth,
From people in Africa with no food,
To fathers abusing mothers and being very rude.

For them it feels as if Christmas never came,
Year after year it's always the same,
No trees, no gifts and no Christmas lights,
Behind some closed doors only bloodshed and fights.

The greatest gift they have is their lives,
Bruised and battered are some wives,
Christmas is meant to bring harmony and peace,
Some end up dead like the geese.

For some they get the Christmas they've always seeked,
No tears or blood are ever leaked,
A lot of lucky people get away,
For they live to see another Christmas Day.

Amy Clift

CHRISTMAS JOY

The moon is lifting in the bright night sky
The air is cold, frost is out to bite
Little children peering out of windows and doors
Trying to catch a glimpse
Of the wonderful Santa Claus
The man who is going to make all their dreams come true
With one drop in the night just for me and you
Trays of mince pies await this special man
Milk for his reindeers, if you can.

Listening for his sleigh bells
As they nod off to sleep
Dreaming he's in the room with them
Instead of counting sheep
Their laughter in the morning
As they open all their gifts
A joyous sound that fills the air
And gives a special lift.

Christmas is a wonderful time
Let's enjoy it so
All we need to make it perfect
Is a covering of snow!

Ruth Fellows

A CHRISTMAS REVELATION 2004

Gazing through the church window,
The nativity scene caught my eye.
A mother nursing her baby,
Heart-warming sensation, which conveyed a sigh.

Pride in the mother's celestial pose,
Created emotional interest, adorning love,
A sign to be sure,
'Yes', a heavenly message, from above.

A mother's love, for her long awaited child,
Flowed from her being,
Contentment shone from her eyes, expressed with holy meaning.

God's gift of a child, whether humble, or holy,
Credits a lifetime legacy, cherishing, devotedly.
Foundations of love, to care and share,
Anchorage of life, wisdom's philosophy, none to compare.

I gazed through the church window once again,
To welcome the honour, I recognised, through the pane,
A gift we can all relate to, on Christmas Day,
The birthday of *Jesus*, in whose mother's arms, He lay.

Lorna Tippett

THE MEANING OF CHRISTMAS

Is it nothing to you,
all you who pass by,
that Christ came to Earth
from His glory on high?

You see trees and Santas,
mince pies and bright lights,
but what's the real reason
for joy on this night?

We think of the baby
so snug in the hay
and give thanks to God
for that first Christmas Day.

Diana Lynch

CHRISTMAS OF GOODWILL

Christmas is of goodwill
Goodwill and all men
Men and say us boys
Boys of eight, nine or ten
Ten and say older
Want designer stuff
If of not designer
Upturned nose and duff
Duff is of commercial
Commercial Christmas now
Now and of always
Always but so much now.

Michael D Bedford

THE CHRISTMAS LOTTERY

She knew the pleasures Christmas brought,
A hoard of gifts beneath the tree.
Her senses dulled, debased by wealth,
She did not know her soul was free.

She knew the dirt beneath her feet,
Haunted eyes, too numb to cry.
Her senses dulled by pain and grief,
She did not know her soul could fly.

The child indulged, the child forsaken.
Cries of joy, cries of pain.
2000-year-old lessons forgotten,
Mankind divided by greed and gain.

Righteousness smothered in tinsel and glitter,
Dishonouring the child who was laid in a manger.
Peace and goodwill to all who can buy it,
Christ forsaken, Christ the stranger.

Frances Roberts

ARBOREAL SANTA

Red with green doesn't always mean;
Christmas.
I have a red-leafed tree,
tall between two green ones,
in my garden, and,
they don't give me that 5-year-old's uncontrollable grin,
that seeing snow,
and hearing 'Jingle Bells',
does.

Megan Davies

A Homeless Christmas - From Me

We are just, kids on the street
Just, wishing for a family to meet
To take care of us, feed us
Not let us down, to just be there.

To always be around, when we are worrying
To listen to us, instead of hurrying
Past, just like you do
You don't have a clue, do you?

I'm sitting on the floor
I won't take much more
Of your space, as I know you are late
To get your Christmas turkey and dates.

I'm sorry I annoyed you, by asking for money
I've been kicked out of my home! *I'm all alone!*
If I had a mobile too, I'd pick up the phone
But then, I remember! I have no home.

It's only me
I'm sorry I disturbed you
It just wasn't meant to be
A happy life for me.

Karen Ferrari

BLOOMIN' CHRISTMAS

Christmas planning for Christmas presents and food,
Christmas shopping puts the ladies in the Christmas mood.
Christmas carols sung at the Christmas garden centre,
Christmas has started it's the end of September.

Christmas cards sent with much Christmas cheer,
Christmas spirit drunk with plenty of Christmas beer.
Christmas presents tied with sparkly Christmas strings,
Christmas toys for the children's Christmas stockings.

Christmas turkey for our roasted Christmas dinner,
Christmas pudding is a certain Christmas winner.
Christmas trifle with lashings of Christmas sherry,
Christmas films slumped in front of the Christmas telly.

Christmas chocolates and even more Christmas sweets,
Christmas bicycles ridden down quiet Christmas streets.
Christmas tree adorned with tinsel and Christmas lights,
Christmas cake to 'just top you up' on Christmas night.

Christmas family gatherings and friends' Christmas get together,
Christmas rain, not the mythical snowy Christmas weather.
After so many weeks talking of all these Christmas matters,
It's a surprise we're not absolutely *Christmas crackers!*

Steve Cannon

THANK YOU MAMA

Sweet Mama,
On whom the Yes was fulfilled.
The Lord's best handmaid,
Who accepted without compromise.
Thank you Mama!
Mary, Our Special Lady.
For that part in our Redemption,
Well played with heart and soul.
By obedience and Gabriel's word,
You conceived.
Thank you Mama!
Dear Virgin Mother.
For nine months,
Whose chaste womb God's son
Dwelt in peacefully.
Your faith holds wide open the doors of hope.
Thank you Mama!
Mama, our charity Queen.
Remember us on this pilgrimage below.
Guide us to your son
So that our joys may be complete.
Thank you Mama!

Nyasha John Musimwa

A SAVIOUR'S BIRTH

Into a carpenter's family He quietly came
A small holy child, Christ Jesus His name.
No room for the birth in Bethlehem's inns
For a babe who was sent to die for our sins.
There was no announcement, no sound of a horn,
Just a cold, dusty stable where our Saviour was born.
His mother, a virgin, His father was God
His home was the land where David had trod.
The shepherds were summoned from tending their sheep
To visit the manger and the infant in sleep.
And kings came with homage from strange lands afar
Led by the beams of a bright, glowing star.
So now we remember this on Christmas Day
That God sent His Son to show us the way.

Bob Pierce

CHRISTMAS 2004

Imagine dust and desert sand blowing, in place of drifting snow,
Flies and mosquitoes everywhere buzzing, no pretty mistletoe.

Burning sunshine instead of icy dragon's breath,
Walking miles and miles hoping for just one crumb of Red Cross bread.

Empty bellies rumbling, no, it's not a festive song,
Cries of an African nation whose children won't live long.

Twenty years on we're still sticking Band-Aids on,
Gaping wounds that need real healing, political medicine.

Twenty years on, they should be celebrating,
Not still dying in their thousands empty bellied, starving hungry.

Barbara Balmer

Santa's Christmas

Rudolph and co have a sleigh to heave
They pull Santa and a sack full of toys on Christmas Eve.
Father Christmas usually takes all of the praise
But most of the time he's in a daze.
His little helpers run the grotto,
They have to, he's always blotto.
Too many mince pies and glasses of sherry
All go to make him merry.
Nick says it's rude to refuse refreshment left on a table,
Pies and drinks, marked for Santa on a label.
Santa can be noisy as he bumps into chairs,
Trips over rugs, then falls down the stairs.
The amount of time stuck up a chimney is anyone's guess
Elves follow him around cleaning up his mess.
How he gets away with it fills me with awe
As he staggers, and stumbles out through the door.
Reindeers outside hovering on the air
As out pops Santa into Rudolph's glare.
Elves and fairies are there to assist
That's because he's always Brahms and List.
It will soon be over then back to the North Pole
He's out of work now, time to claim the dole.
He can relax and look forward to next year,
For eleven months stay off the beer.
He must diet and lose several pounds
Until once again do the rounds.
We all love Santa in his suit so red
From the bottom of his boots to the top of his head.
So long Santa, long may you rule,
Ho, ho, ho, have a cool Yule.

Patricia Whorwood

CHRISTMAS LOVE AND LIGHT

Christmas is a time of love
That comes from Heaven above
Jesus was born a long time ago
In a manger as we all know
The wise men came to visit Him so
A star showed them where to go
They gave him gold, frankincense and myrrh
He came down to save many souls
To heal the sick and the old
So much love for His fold
He taught His disciples what to do
As he said, 'I'll not always be with you'
He taught the Christian Kabbalah
And the tree of life too
The light came to us too
Spiritual light white yellow and blue
This is what Christmas is about too
The light and love that shines inside us too
If you practise this too
The spiritual world is there for you
You don't have to be a Christian or Jew
If you are its Christ conscience
Or even Jesus will do
The light of love will shine on you

Gordon Forbes

CHRISTMAS EVE

It's Christmas Eve, the church bells ring
And my thoughts go in the past
Did our dear Lord hear our prayers
And send us help at last.

In a manger we did find
A gift from God, a little boy
And all the wise men went to see
Dear Mary's love and joy.

In the sky, one star stood out
And on the manger it did shine
To show us where His son was born
To share with us His love divine.

I made my way from the church
Through the snow all crisp and white
I said my prayers and thanked the Lord
For Christmas Eve, a special night.

A F Mace

ANOTHER CHRISTMAS TIME

Christmas time,
Had too much wine
Family wages war at nine
With the turkey on fire
Pine needles falling off the tree
I pretend to rejoice at the gifts given to me.

David Woods

The Night That Santa Comes

Can't wait for Father Christmas to come, I hope that he's got my letter,
I have been behaving myself this year, well at least I have been better,
I asked him for a bicycle, some books and more games to play as well,
I was even a bit cheeky, and asked if on my bike he would put a bell.

Well, 'Don't ask, don't get,' at least that's what Mum says to my dad,
It always seems to work for her, for last time Santa came she had,
Some really flashy jewellery, a coat and something that I could not see,
Apparently it was a naughty little number that was tucked
inside the tree.

I wonder how Santa gets down the chimney, with all he has to bring,
And how Rudolph never wakes me, yet his sleigh bells surely ring,
He is a clever man, and I think that my mum knows him personally.
She leaves him out a mince pie and some beer, rather than a cup of tea?

What I find strange is that all the cupboards are locked at this
time of year,
And instead of talking loudly, I find my parents very difficult to hear,
It's as if there is some secret, that for some reason I am not to know,
Who cares, I only hope that on Christmas morning I wake up
to some snow.

On Christmas Eve, I go to bed and my parents check to see
if I am asleep,
I pretend that I am, but something strange is going on, as
around they creep,
Are they playing some kind of game? Perhaps they are excited
just like me,
Can't wait till I wake up in the morning, to see what presents are
by the tree.

I think I hear some rustling of paper whilst I lie in my
semi-conscious state,
I think that it must be Rudolph, who is probably standing out there
by the gate,
Mum leaves him out a carrot each year, something to crunch on,
so they say,
But he was not very hungry last year because in the hearth half of it lay.

I must have fallen off to sleep, because I wake to light shining
through my room,
And I can hear the sound of somebody in the street, sweeping
with a broom,
I look out of my window and can't believe what I see out there
in the street,
There is a sea of snow covering the roofs and roads and there must
be several feet.

I rush towards Mum and Dad, and then race downstairs to make
sure he's been,
There's a pile of presents just waiting there, perhaps more than I have
ever seen,
I can't wait to get started, but am concerned that there is nothing that
looks like,
The present I really want, 'Oh Santa, did you remember to
bring my bike?'

Mum and Dad come down the stairs, and I think they can see
I am not right,
And Dad goes straight outside to the garden, in fact he is now
out of sight,
This is no time for a walk, is he OK, perhaps he is not feeling very well,
But suddenly I can hear this familiar noise, and it sounds like a
bicycle bell.

Santa did remember, but why did he leave this present out there in the shed?
Surely he could have brought it inside by coming through the door instead,
Never mind, it's here and yet again he must have received my letter,
You see I told you that this year, I have been behaving myself better!

Christmas comes but once a year, and it is a time when we should all be merry,
Including Granny who gets just a little tipsy when she has more than one sherry,
Crackers are pulled, jokes are told and in the afternoon we sit down by the telly.
While Santa takes off his boots and gown, and sits and rests with his full belly.

Mark Jacobs

CHRISTMAS 2001

Christmas is coming, the geese are getting fat,
Please put some money in a little red hat.
Santa is preparing for the long night ahead,
All the elves are working in their big shed.
Getting presents ready for all the girls and boys,
For when Santa comes with all the toys.

After the long night, Santa is tired,
He sits in front of a large log fire,
To rest his weary self and wonders, *do I retire?*
No of course not, the children would miss me.
It wouldn't be Christmas without me!

Marian Clark

CHRISTMAS

In the towns the people hustle.
The Morris dance.
The buskers bustle.
In the towns the people hurry.
The army plays.
The snowflakes flurry.
In the towns the people race.
The needy starve.
The cold embrace.
In the towns the people run.
The lonely cry.
The Mass begun.
In the towns the people stare.
The beggar dies.
No one to care.
In our heads the pressures rise.
In our heart an angel sighs.
In a room somewhere a baby cries.
An angry man in a fit of pique
Hurts a child so mild and meek.
Gentle sobs from a stone-cold bed,
Mother strokes his tiny head.
The bad man in the corner's here,
Blessed we shed a silent tear.
Daylight brings no Christmas fair.
Don't ask why, you wouldn't dare.
No shoes upon their wretched feet.
No steaming pud, nor turkey meat.
No toys or games or doll or train,
But Father's down the pub again.

Bill Surman

NOEL AU PAI'S #8221 (CHRISTMAS IN THE HOMELAND)

At Christmas time, the sight of Mother's lovely head gently bent
over the crate,
Where her figurines had lain dormant throughout the year, readying
them for the crèche,
Appeared just as wondrous a sight as the infant child being laid amidst
the hay,
And brings back memories of the first lesson I learned as to the
meaning of the season.
While I watched her work, fascinated by the lifelike quality of the
manger scene,
I would lean over to touch the figurines, anticipating rebuke,
Feeling compelled to participate in what she was doing, I asked her
to explain.
An expression of divine love she called it, letting me experience
the magic.
Later on, as I walked with her, hand in hand after the midnight mass,
Many more questions I asked, while enjoying the cool, crisp night air.
She told me of a God, whose love affair with human race is
never-ending.
Watching the stars in their magnificent luminosity, I tried to picture
the baby Jesus,
Rendered speechless by the swelling gratitude for the love she so
reverently described.
Years later when I try to absorb the notion of a divine birth
precursory to the sacrifice,
I found so much beauty and grace so freely lavished too wonderful
to comprehend.
A feeling that continues to overwhelm me and take my breath away.
I feel the wonder of years past coming back each Christmas,
bringing with it the same sense of awe,
Rendering me eternally grateful for the gift that secures me
a permanent place in Heaven.

Gladys Bruno

MESSIAH

No tinsel, tree or coloured lights
No gift-wrapped presents, no invites
Just another naked birth
A pile of straw, a smell of earth

No announcements in the press
No silver spoon, no silken dress
Just a shed where cattle feed
Amid the tools and bags of seed.

No kings or queen to bow and scrape
No cardinals, no golden cape
Just another anxious mum
A worried dad, a hungry son.

No angel choir, no trumpet call
No blazing star, the sign for all
Just flies and wind across the plain
Man's welcome to the human game.

No haloed heads, lambs breathing hard
No kneeling shepherds keeping guard
Just words in books, a rhyming feast
Cathedral choir, a smiling priest.

No Holy Night, no Little Town
No glamour Mum in fashion gown
Just dirt and smell and fear and cold
That's all the story ever told.

Brian Henry

SKIPPING CHRISTMAS

Every year the same old story,
Christmas comes with all its glory.

Rushing round the shops and stores,
up the stairs and through the doors.

Fighting crowds and getting tense,
none of this makes any sense.

Then the day with too much food
puts me in a stroppy mood.

Now my house is in a state,
I'm far too tired to put it straight.

And so this year I have a plan,
we'll go away, me and my man.

We'll leave the kids, the dog, the cat,
whatever will they think of that?

When Christmas comes we'll stay in bed,
we'll just eat crisps and cheese and bread.

And drink and love and watch TV,
on everything we will agree.

And then if luck still shines our way,
we'll get snowed in and have to stay.

Oh what a truly blissful plan,
I'll make it work, I know I can.

My happy thoughts I'll not suppress,
life's just too short for all this stress.

Muriel Nicola Waldt

CHRISTMAS

Tinsel and baubles,
Food and drink,
Bright lights and Christmas trees,
Happy, singing, laughing,
Rejoicing in life.
Mince pies and cookies,
Santa Claus dressed in red,
Presents under Christmas trees,
Christmas cards and money.

Pots and beds,
No food or water,
Smell of sweat and bodies,
Crying babies, swearing,
No hope for new life.
Hard work without end,
Streets dressed in red,
Dead grass under dead trees,
Stolen money, stolen life.

Straw and hay,
Donkey and sheep,
Bright star and stable,
Baby crying, mother laughing,
Rejoicing in new life.
Shepherd and wise man,
Little boy to dress in red,
Presents foretell future,
To give back stolen life.

Ceri Siân

CHRISTMAS WISH

I don't want more toys this year, the ones I have will do,
I don't want clothes, mine are good, so I'll cope with them too.
I don't want any sweets this year, we have enough to eat,
No, I don't want books, or tapes, or games, I don't need those
types of treats.

What I want this year, is not that at all, in fact it's not even a thing,
Yet the one thing I want is the hardest to find, nothing that Santa
can bring.
What I long for this Christmas, is love from the heart, a love: strong
and bold, true and real,
From anyone, anywhere, I really don't care, all I want is a love
that is real.

I have so much stuff, others do but dream of, power and money galore,
The world thinks I'm lucky, but that stuff is worthless, happiness means
so much more.
You can have all that I have, new books and new games, CDs a brand
new doll or toy,
But money and toys - they don't mean a thing, it's love that gives
you joy.

That's the thing I want this Christmas, forget all the wealth and
acclaim.
I'll give anything, everything, all that I own, if I can have love
just the same.

Victoria Morley (13)

CHRISTMAS

C is for Christmas, carols and cheer
   Wishing us joy at this time of year

H is for holly with its berries so bright
   Decking our houses for the children's delight

R is for ringing the church bells this day
   Calling us to church as we go on our way

I is for icing on the Christmas cake
   With a drop of sherry, we all partake

S is for snow, making everything white
   Changing the landscape, a beautiful sight.

T is for tinsel on the presents we see
   Waiting to be opened, under the tree

M is for Mary at this holy birth
   Jesus, the Christ-child has come down to Earth

A is for ass in the stable forlorn
   His breath on the baby, keeping Him warm

S is for Saviour on the day He was born
   The reason we celebrate this glad Christmas morn

Barbara M Beatson

CHRISTMAS

Christmas as you know
Comes but once a year
Old adage I know
You've guessed, I hear

You see the friends
Not seen for so long
But come the New Year
Will once again, they be gone?

It's good for friends
To always keep in touch
Once known for many a year
Might you miss them so much?

Christmas for many people
Can be a time a lonely
Never think of yourself
Never think of you only

What we give out it is said
Tenfold the joy we get back
If you're doing something,
Do it for others, for those
With so much lack.

Simone C Summerscales

CHRISTMAS

Yuletide logs and mistletoe,
Blazing fires and hearts aglow,
Trees bedecked with lights and holly,
Christmas cards and carols, jolly;
Jingle bells on Santa's sleigh,
Happiness that's here to stay;
Children bursting with delight,
Cannot sleep on Christmas night;
Snowflakes falling all around,
Lying pristine, on the ground;
Sparkling frost with icy hand;
Turns to winter wonderland;
Bitter wind to howl and chill,
Through the hours so dark and still;
Twinkling star, that shines so bright,
Lending magic to the night;
Silent moon shines over all,
Ox and ass, in stable small,
Wise men with their gifts to bring,
In honour of the newborn King,
Little child of mystery,
Sent to Earth for you and me,
Lying in a bed of straw,
Fills us with a sense of awe;
Do you know you are the reason
For this joy, the festive season?

Dorothy Neil

STAR CHILDREN

The sky was bright,
Moon washed with clouds
High in a dome of darkest blue,
The Heavens were high and soared
Into the vastness of other worlds,
Out of view.

On the snow waiting Earth
There was a dearth of colour,
Everything was shadowed in winter,
And then the star children
Unveiled their glittering faces,
And from their places.
Looked down to see
What they could,
Out of eternity.

They had seen the first Christmas,
The stable, the shepherds,
The travelling kings,
Watched the hosts of angels,
Heard them sing.

They had shone from the beginning
As the world grew,
And knew that from eternity,
What was promised in the stable
Was true.

D M Neu

AN ANGEL OF THE LORD

Some sing,
O Come, O Come, Emmanuel.

Some busy themselves
inside shopping malls,
while others muse
amongst the tinselled stalls.

Children gather
around Christmas grottos -
a picturesque place
that's more than a dream,
Father Christmas
sits on a scarlet throne.

Children throng
to hear the story foretold,
with the haltered donkey
and gifts threefold.

Gentle child sleeps
before gallant men -
elongated shadows
in orange glow.

A new star was born,
and was shining bright -
like a diamond,
set in black velvet night.

Olliver Charles

What Is Christmas?

Come tell me, what is Christmas all about?
When you go out shopping, you hear everyone shout.
Apples a pound, pears, or Christmas trees,
Cheap at the price, why not have three?
Down in the market, fruit and veg stalls,
Prices so different, it makes you pall.

Into the toy shop for decorations,
Dolls and prams, tanks and guns.
Baby dolls your little daughter wants,
The boys want trains to shunt.
Prices usually too dear for you to pay,
Telling the kids you'll come back next day.

Decorations for trees and tinsel to hang,
You must have crackers with a lovely bang.
Santa Claus suits for Christmas party
Everyone will be hale and hearty.
Plenty of wine and spirits flow,
Some have too much as they cannot go slow.

Christmas cake and mince pies too,
So much turkey you don't know what to do.
Yet how many think why we have Christmas days,
Very few ever think what the Lord says.
He gave His son for the redemption of men,
That's what we should remember again and again.

Disown those that are grasping and take everything,
The misers and skinflints from the Devil's domain.
Love thy neighbour; take care of your friends,
For some day you'll need them, when nearing your end.

Ken Copley

CHRISTMAS CARDS

What happens
to Christmas
cards when
you die?
Do they still
keep on coming?
Or do they stop
when they get
no reply?
Good wishes with
no home to
go to.
Merriness unrequited;
cherubs invalidated.

Colin Shaw

CHRISTMAS TREE

A
Christmas tree
Is a wondrous sight
With pretty flashing lights
Decked and adorned
For all to see
Be-ribboned presents for you
And for me. Angels, snowmen, reindeer
Tinsel and tempting chocolates; Santa Claus
Take time to admire and pause
Baby
Jesus
Is the
Cause

Theresa M Carrier

THE OLD GREY BALL

Every Christmas they go to their beds
Every Christmas I'm locked in the shed
The children are waiting in sheer delight
What will arrive on this magical night?

Computers, new trainers, keyboard and games?
I feel neglected to say the least
But then God's will is a time of peace.

Children playing, frost at their feet
Kicking a ball down the street
I had this!
I had that!
I got this!
I got that!

After Christmas, what do they do?
Kick an old ball down the street
Ears tingling, noses red
Put the old ball back in the shed.
Back to the warmth, everything new
The old grey ball is waiting for you.

Children are happy, full of content
Presents and happiness all of the day.
Let's share with the ones who did not
Computers, trainers, keyboards not got.

I have an idea, let's open the shed
Ears tingling, noses red.
Laughter and happiness down the street
The old grey ball is out to greet.

C Umpleby

A Christmas Message

Greetings
Cheery meetings
Kisses and embraces
Leaving rosy lipstick traces
Are all enjoyed each Yuletide.
Family gatherings, festive occasions, tearful reunions,
Carol singing, Christmas shopping and prayerful communions
All collectively create the ambience of Christmas time.
Our own seasonal regards to flow to every family member
And friend, as goodwill is expressed sincerely again in December.
These warm and heartfelt wishes for Christmas we happily send
Worldwide.
Merry
Christmas
Everyone

Allen Jessop

Christmas

I send my love for Christmas
And like you all to think
Although love is not shown
There is a special link
Mother's, Father's love we share
And within our hearts
Is always there
And love for all
We keep and share
God be with you
With love and care.

Pat Jakes

A SPECIAL CHRISTMAS VISITOR

I have a little story
I'd like to tell to you, you likely won't believe it
But I do assure you it's true.

'Twas the night before Christmas, all the wrapping was done,
The presents were under the tree, it really looked so pretty
And the fairy was smiling at me.

With a feeling of great satisfaction I sat back in the chair to relax,
I poured myself a wee Baileys, to sip and enjoy, just perhaps.

When all of a sudden I was startled, I heard a great thump on the roof
And a deep booming voice shouting, 'Whoa there.'
Was this to be my proof?

Now we don't have a chimney, not many have these days,
Was I about to find out, the secret of Santa's ways?

He knocked up on the door and then came bounding in,
'Hello my dear, how are you? I just popped in on a whim.'

We sat in our comfy armchairs, on either side of the fire,
Sipped a glass of warming sherry,
While Santa contentedly patted his spare tyre.

'I've many miles to cover, on this most magical of nights,
And if you have the time, why not come see the sights?'

We climbed upon the roof and sped off on his sleigh,
His reindeer were all galloping, taking us on our merry way.

And long into the night, over rooftops glistening with snow,
He delivered all his presents, to the children far below.

I think I was very privileged to be shown how his magic is spun,
I had to say my goodbyes to Santa in the rising of a cold, crispy dawn.

He dropped me off on my doorstep, so I planted a kiss on his cheek,
You can believe me when I tell you the last thing I wanted was sleep.

So to all you non-believers, please listen I know I am right,
Santa Claus is definitely out there!
I travelled with him and his reindeer last night.

Margaret M Donnelly

THE CHRISTMAS SNOWMAN

Mr Snowman come and see
What they've done to the garden tree
It's full of baubles . . . reds and blues
And a bright, shiny star for all to view.

Mr Snowman come and see
All the people by the tree
Hear the voices sing out loud
Such a happy, joyous crowd.

Mr Snowman come and see
Lots of presents round the tree
Read the labels, untie the bows
Who they're for . . . I don't know.

So Mr Snowman it's been such fun
But watch out now here comes the sun.
And as you slowly melt away
I'll see you again on the next Christmas Day.

Linda Francis

MY THINGAMAJIG

Dear Santa,
I don't know what to do
I think I've broken my thingymjig, it's turned big and blue
I pulled, tugged it, after giving it a jerk
No matter how I try, I can't get the thing to work
My thingymjig is my pride and joy
Now I'm not a happy little boy
I've wrapped it in cottonwool; and gave it loving, tender care
But I cannot fix it, it's just not fair
This is why Santa, I write you this letter
In the hope you can make things better
Please send me a new thingymjig as soon as you can
Yours truly
Johnny (aged seven, an unhappy little man)

Terry J Powell

SAME DAY, DIFFERENT YEAR

Her eyes light up, as bright as those on the tree.
Standing proud for all to see.
A reminder of previous Christmas glee.
Her smiles, her joy at all to see
with her family and friends what a pleasure it will be.
Our family's home is where we are heading,
my daughter and I.
A different Christmas this year
than the few she has seen.
We hope for love and fun, a peaceful new year,
no more reminders of what could have been.

Karen Roberts

BAUBLES

I like baubles;
I like their bright colours
Shining on a dull winter day,
Catching the light;
Red, gold, silver, green, blue;
Round, dome-shaped, pointed,
They look exotic and eastern,
More as if they originated in Turkey than Germany.
Even the word 'bauble' conjures up images
Of caliphs and sultans in turned-up slippers,
Flying through the air on magic carpets;
Wise men in turbans, riding richly dressed camels
Laden with gold, frankincense and myrrh
Spring to mind as I decorate the Christmas tree.

Kathy Rawstron

CHRISTMAS CHEER

Christmas comes just once a year
When it comes it brings good cheer
Christmas is a time for fun
Christmas is for everyone
Come on children, let me hear you sing
Come on children, let your voices ring
Christmas is a time for love
Get on your knees to the Lord above
Christmas is a time for prayer
Christmas is a time to share
Come on children let me hear you sing
Come on children let your voices ring
Christmas is a time to give
For the young children in Africa to live.

H G Booley

CHRISTMAS SHOPPING

People shopping, never stopping
In and out the store
Pavement hopping, brows-a-mopping
Feet and legs are sore

Children skipping, falling, tripping
Flat upon the floor
Noses dripping, hands-a-gripping
Making for the door

Onions smelling, vendors selling
Traffic at full roar
Time is telling, tears are welling
Soon be half-past four

Light is failing, children wailing
Feel you've fought a war
Taxi hailing, past you sailing
Really the last straw!

Jackie Johnson

CHRISTMAS POEM

Christmas comes and Christmas goes,
Nearly lost the feeling.
Christmas cheer and snowflake's song,
Almost gone, was any meaning,
But this year, this one's different,
Today the warmth is true,
Someone made my Christmas special,
Just wanted to say, 'Thank you!'

Sarah Heptinstall

SONG FOR THE CHILDREN

When I look at windows as I walk by from the street
Their soft glow shining through the windowpane
I wonder what lives live behind the Christmas scene
And if Christmas is rich or really plain

I wonder what the children see, is it happiness and cheer
Or is it all drunkenness and fear
Is it presents, Christmas morning and a big breakfast spread
Or is it all cold, damp and dead?

I pray for every child this Christmas, wherever they may be
That they will find warmth and happiness
And whether they have plenty, or their home is very bare
The *Lord* will be with each of them and bless.

Grace Divine

MOTHER AND BABY, FINE

If God indeed came down that day
and as an infant, meekly lay
between the beasts, on bed of hay,
there in a feeder, in a stall,
2 kilograms, yet God of all.
Then that event should doubtless be
far greater than some Christmas tree,
the tinsel, food, the gifts, the gloss,
and all the tat that is or was
built into every Christmas time
with all its gluttony and wine.
Far better we should stop in awe
at what they say those shepherds saw.

Richard Stead

CHRISTMAS WORDS . . . WHILST SHOPPING
(A 21st century Christmas tale)

So I said to the homeless guy . . .

Would you like to share Christmas with my hubby and me,
In our costly little one bedroom abode?

He said . . .
No thanks, my dog and I are happy sharing rent free in our W1 zone.

I said . . .
But don't your evenings fall cold with the dark of the night?

He said . . .
No! We sleep under the warmth and the glitter of the Oxford St lights.

I said . . .
Christmas for us was downbeat from the start.

He said . . .
That's because Christmas doesn't live in your heart.

Jessie Morton

UNTITLED

Wrap the presents,
Trim the tree.
Lots of gifts,
For you and me.
Sing some carols,
Eat fruit cake.
The things we do
For Christmas' sake.

Jay Berkowitz

SOMETHING SPECIAL AT CHRISTMAS

Something special is my sister,
my sister had a 'Twister'
then had a blister on her big toe.

Fun at Christmas is great
Christmas, Christmas trees are green, winter spells
are coming now, Christmas is nearer and dearer.

Church bells are ringing,
carol singers are singing.

Christmas is near,
Christmas is here.
Christmas is my best time of year.

Hannah Ryan (9)

JINGLE ALL THE WAY

Oh what I feel about Christmas
is more than anything in the world.
It is good at Christmas,
just as a robin bird.
You see when it's Christmas,
the snow falls down, like the rain.
And when it is next Christmas
it will happen again and again.
Santa will come in, isn't that nice,
it is just like water dripping from the ice.
Oh what I feel about Christmas is yippee, yippee!
Because all the snow is for you and me.

Joanna Lloyd-Barrett (9)

CHRISTMAS TIME

Winter comes at Christmas
With the north wind which blows
Bringing with it rain and snow.
We look in the eastern sky
And see the Bethlehem star
Which comes at Christmas
Also. We go to old club parties
And send Christmas cards and presents
To friends and relations.
We listen to carol singers,
Also hear the church bell ring out
To invite us to midnight service
To celebrate Jesus' birth.
We celebrate the joy of Christmas
And wish everyone good tidings
For the New Year.

A F Hiscocks

POEM TO SANTA

Dear Santa,
Please bring me . . .

Button men, candy sticks and clothes galore
Chocolate, cakes, turkey and lots more
Happiness and fun, all in a bag
Presents wrapped up, 'From Santa' on a tag
Teddy bears and instruments that make a sound
Nibbles and parcels passed around
Christmas carols and words filling my ears
Perfume for Mum and for Dad, tins of beers
Visiting friends and family
A fun-filled Christmas for you and for me.

Katie Richards (11)

WHAT IS CHRISTMAS?

Christmas is time for caring and sharing,
Remembering friends who are far away.
Giving fresh hope to those downhearted,
Love and our help on Christmas Day.
Spreading the wondrous Christmas message,
Given to man from Heaven above,
Jesus is born in a humble stable,
Come with the gift of heavenly love.
Follow the star that led the wise men,
Let it lead us to Bethlehem,
Come and let us all adore Him,
As we go and follow them.
Leave behind the noise and tumult
Of man's quarrels, war and strife,
Come and let us kneel before Him
Promise of eternal life . . .

Margaret B Baguley

CHRISTMAS

I'm lost in the reverie and unbelievable magic of Christmas.
I bought my princess (wife) a secret Santa gift.
As the fire crackles with warmth and a distant fading in and out,
I relax from all the hustle and bustle.
It's good to relax.
The constancy of Christmas is settling for me.
The wife worked the second shift this day,
So I wrapped up the tree decorations -
The house needed fine tuning.
Outside it's so cold, the breath freezes in the air.
But inside there is a special holiday warmth.

Colin Zarhett

CHRISTMAS

It happens every single year
Don't go blamin' Santa
Stock the fridge wae wine and beer
Crispy snacks and Fanta

Chicken wings and chocolate things
Pies and cream and brussels
Soup and cheese wae lots o' grease
Great big jars o' mussels

Tons o' chips and spicy dips
Ice cream on a platter
Sickly sweets and potted meats
Guess who's getting fatter?

Swill it roon and pour it doon
Hear yer belly rumble
There's a space so hurry, race
'Gie's some rhubarb crumble.'

Plates o' ham and strawb'ry jam
Butter oan a muffin
Turkey legs and boiled eggs
Don't forget the stuffin'.

Roasted tatties, extra peas
Cover it wae gravy
Extra helpings . . . 'Oh yes please.'
(This would feed the navy)

Now you want to have a sleep
Lie doon on the soaffy
Couldn'y eat another thing
'How about a coffee?

Surely you could force wan doon
Wae a gin and tonic?'
Pickled onions, fat cigars
Now yer breath is chronic.

Wan mair brandy then a beer
The calories are loadin'
And whit's that noise ye all can hear,
Why that's yer bum explodin'!

Now it's over, all is past
You feel as rich as Croesus
Wan thing you forgot tae ask,
'Who the hell is Jesus?'

Franz

CHRISTMAS

Christmas trees with tinsel and baubles
fairy lights twinkling so bright
Holly wreaths with vivid red berries
hung on doors make a welcoming sight.

Roast turkey with trimmings, plum pudding and bonbons
a meal that is fit for a king
In churches we gather to praise Jesus' birth
and carols we joyfully sing.

Stockings hung up to be filled by old Santa
he travels the world on a sleigh
To deliver on time, with his reindeer to help him
before nightfall breaks into day.

More presents of all shapes and sizes
lovingly placed under the tree
All wrapped with care, for the family to share
in colours of gold, red and green.

Snow softly falling, it blankets the grass
and adds to the joy of a happy Christmas.

Joyce Smith

CHRISTMAS CELEBRATION

The Christmas celebration
Brings joyful elation
To one and all.
Everyone is extra kind,
Peace is wished for all mankind
Because of the baby
Born and placed in a manger stall.

We fill our homes with decorations,
Send cards to friends and relations
For peace and joy.
Gifts are placed around a tree,
Carols are sung in harmony
Remembering the birth
Of Jesus Christ that baby boy.

Joan Earle Broad

HAPPY HOLY DAYS

Especially at Christmas and all through the year
It's important to touch those who you hold dear

Responsibilities, obligations and events of life
Leave impressions on us of nothing but strife

In light of all this we can expect to pull through
With loving kindness, God, and help from people like you

Remember the Holy Spirit and keep it in your heart
The new year goes better if it's with you from the start

May the Spirit bring realisation of goals you have set
And dreams for the ones you have not thought of yet.

Mary Cathleen Brown

UNTITLED

Christmas is here, a time of great joy
smiles on the faces of each girl and boy.
Presents all sitting waiting under the tree
this one's for you, this one's for me.
But do we stop amidst all this joy,
to give a thought to one special boy,
born in a stable in a country far away?
Surely this is His special day.
So enjoy all the parties, the feasting and wine
but busy as you may be, please try to find time
to think of that manger, the baby and star
and the three kings who came from afar.
Without all of these wonderful things
we would not have Christmas.
So let us sing to the glory above
and try to fill this world with our love.

S Pritchard

HOMECOMING

Christmas in our homes and hearts
A welcome at our door:
An atmosphere of love and peace
And happy times in store . . .
A glittering tree and fire bright
With warmth surround the guest,
His family assembled here
Bring Christmas happiness . . .
Season of goodwill and hope
Bring us these precious gifts,
A spirit of contentment and joy
Which our soul uplifts!

Carolyn Smith

THE PATIENCE OF GOD

God waited 'til the time was right
For Jesus to be born.
He could have sent him years before,
The world was then forlorn.
But no! God's timing had to be
The moment of his choice,
When Roman roads were being built
And Greek the common voice.

God waiteth yet! Though Jesus came
To live upon this Earth,
Its people still reject God's way
And faith comes not to birth.
But wait! God's patience runs not out -
His love for all holds firm.
As Christmas comes around once more
May more to Jesus turn.

Geoffrey T Perry

BABY

A baby changes a household
A baby changes the world -
Joseph was a new man
New by the child he fathered
Mary carried the future
Delivered her Deliverer -
To Nazareth, a community for nurture
Safe because nobody admits,
Admits they come from there -
Chosen by God to bless the nations.

Irene Clare Garner

LIKE GENTLE SNOW

Like gentle snow that changes all, yet hardly makes a sound,
So baby Jesus came to Earth, and smiled on all around.
No trumpets blared, no bells rang out, no sound of human choirs,
Just ox and ass to welcome Him and shepherds round their fires.

A bed of straw, some walls of stone: a stable dark and bare,
For one who'd come to change the world, were all mankind
                                                                            could spare.
No banquet held as courtiers knelt in robes so rich and fine,
Just patient Joseph tended Him at that first Christmas time.

The baby gazed in Mary's eyes and saw the power of love,
Whilst shimmering in the frosty air, His own star shone above.
No palace heard His infant cries, nor felt His royal tread,
Just king to human shame He'd be, with thorns to crown His head.

Like gentle snow that changes all, yet hardly makes a sound
May this birth fill our hearts with love to spread the world around,
Ensuring that this lowly birth that lit the Middle East
May blaze across the sands of time - this glorious Christmas feast.

Richard J Bradshaw

EARTH'S ANGELS

They tend the Earth, encouraging growth,
With a kind word,
Providing support against life's pitfalls,
Travelling life's journey, helped by kind strangers,
We may never meet again,
But drops of kindness in life's pool,
Whether cut or bruised by society's changes,
There are still angels providing encouragement.

Brian Tallowin

CHRISTMAS IS NOTHING

Christmas is an empty shell
a hollow mountain
a waterless well

Christmas is shallow
and small
has no meaning at all

Christmas may as well
be dismissed
not exist

Without a heart beating
life is nothing
if Christ is missing
Christmas is nothing.

Emma Akuffo

A SAVIOUR IS BORN

A lonely stranger went walking one night,
he saw some lights in a house so bright.
He came to a stable, so bare, and yet there
a baby lay, for all to see.

Shepherds and kings around him did stay,
a star in the sky shone like a diamond above.
The little baby there he lay.

Beyond the hills, so far away,
so long ago this story was told -
before I got old.

Susan Byers

SNOW

Rain turns into snow . . .
I recognised the colour of darkness that touched my eyelids . . .
sometimes . . . when I hide in the thorns as some kind of a wild bird . . .
the palms are full of wounds from the thorn flowers . . .
but feet are not so tired, although running does not have
meaning any longer . . .
Now, at least the wind brings the childhood dreams
and the smell of strawberry.
Suddenly, the taste of hemlock reminds me of the rocky mountains
of pride of some strange people who thought they knew how to think . .
the snow is so familiar . . . swallowing the shreds of the wrestling desire
the purpose of breathing . . .
Snow falls too fast and every time it seems pathetic to cry . . .
but the scars become calm . . .
like purification of pain . . .
sign of something much other than white . . .
a sign.

Jasmina Trifunovic

GIFT OF GIFTS

The festival is alive
with possibilities for
everybody. Love
enters every heart at last.
Laughter is heard
everywhere. Peace enters
the heaviest souls.
Christmas time shakes
the blues away forever.
Happiness is its gift
of gifts.

Kirk Antony Watson

CHRISTMAS

All over the town the lights are shining,
Red and blue and green entwining,
Bringing hope and welcome cheer
At the nadir of the year.

Christmas lights through curtains showing,
Decorated fir trees glowing,
Presents heaped beneath the tree,
All is as it ought to be.

For Christmas is a time of giving,
Makes a pattern in our living,
And families have come from far
To gather where their parents are.

Christmas Day! The bells are ringing.
In the churches, choirs are singing.
Heads are bowed in fervent prayer
For peace and kindness everywhere.

Evelyn Westwood

THE REAL CHRISTMAS

Is Christmas about: carols that we sing?
Or Jesus Christ the Holy King?
Is it: Santa, reindeer, sherry?
Or is it Joseph and his wife Mary?
Is it: presents and decorations?
Or is it Jesus, ruler of the nations?
In all these there is a danger,
We might forget the baby in the manger.
We look forward to Christmas,
But for a moment, just think,
Because with Jesus and Santa there is *no* link!

Benjamin McCanna (10)

CHRISTMAS THROUGH THE EYES OF A CHILD

Christmas through the eyes of a child
Little ones so gentle meek and mild
Babes in awesome wonder watch and wait
While older ones do tend to anticipate.

On Christmas Eve, at night's late hour
With his power Santa brings his shower
Hanging by the fire are children's stockings
Waiting for Santa to come a-knocking.

When comes the dawn on Christmas morn
There may be snow upon the lawn
When the children awake from their sleep
Down the stairs they creep to peep.

'Mum, Dad,' they scream, 'Santa has been.'
To see it's such a wonderful scene
Their faces they are full of smiles
Under the Christmas tree are their piles.

Sophia Cartland

LONELY AT CHRISTMAS

I am lonely at
Christmas
I have no one
To come
I just want
To be loved
For the person
I have become.

Bav

FIDLEYE FEE, FIDLEYE FOE

Fidleye fee, fidleye foe
for it's off to sleep
that you must go

Be hushed of sound
and closed of eye
or St Nicholas won't call tonight

Fidleye fee, fidleye foe
for it's off to sleep
or he shall know

So bed your head
with nothing said
and you'll soon awake
         to a treasure trove!

Simon Knight

A CHRISTMAS FEELING

A special feeling warms me inside
From hope and excitement my soul cannot hide
The smell of mulled wine, the cold winter breeze
The festive carol singers, eager to please
Lovers holding hands, walking in the snow
Sending best wishes to friends I know
Christmas means more than presents to me
This is the time when life's clear to see
The meaning of Christmas is found in your heart
The feeling of love, as the season starts
Everything seems simpler, everyone a friend
This time of goodwill never should end.

Natasha Palmer

CHRISTMAS WISHES

The Christmas lights are shining,
    as this festive time draws near
With peace and heartfelt wonder,
    and the warmth of Christmas cheer

Outside the snow is falling,
    as a crisp cold winter starts
Our children joyfully playing,
    their laughter warms our hearts

In this time for peace on Earth,
    there's no colour, race or skin
But a celebration and joy for life,
    for the love we have within

We wish you all glad tidings,
    for the coming year right through
This merry Christmas message,
    is sent from our hearts to you

Marion McGarrigle

THE ROUND ROBIN LETTER

Please excuse this round robin letter
But it's been such a hectic year.
I've got a new lover - he's a real jet setter.
Please excuse this round robin letter,
I met him in rehab - but now we're both better
And we're off to Columbia for New Year.
Please excuse this round robin letter
But it's been such a hectic year.

Marion Scourfield

HAPPY CHRISTMAS

Season of happiness and good cheer.
Pour me a drink, I'm knackered dear.
Got a banging head, my feet are sore
From scampering round that superstore.

Must stuff the bird, then peel the sprouts.
Stop fighting kids, don't act like louts.
Let's all be cheerful, have a good day.
Nana and Grandad are coming to stay.

Oh there they are now, that's the bell.
Early as always, bloody hell!
So much to do, so little time.
If dinner's late, will it be a crime?

Oh come on in, Happy Christmas to you,
Yes, I think it's a lovely time of year too.

Pam Eaves

DECEMBER DAWN

A cloud studded sky awakes
a new dawn,
Lengthened shadows sprawl
across snow capped lawns;
December's razor sharp winds
cut through to the bone,
Strutting his stuff, a russet-coated
robin, winter's feathered chaperon;
Holly bushes, olive green coats
sport their fiery buttons,
That illuminate the days
that winter shortens.

Peter Morriss

THE SPIRIT OF CHRISTMAS

'What goes around comes around' is ever true
As we send our seasonal blessings to you

What we give, so we receive
No matter what we think or believe

Not just at Christmas or in present form
But all year long should perhaps be the norm

A smile shown here, a friendly word there
Any little gesture to show that we care

The spirit of Christmas is a light within us
Not just on the tree or an ad on a bus

It's not just from Asda that we get Christmas cheer
But also from sharing throughout the long year

So although this comes to you during December
We're sure that you know that we'll always remember!

Keith Beasley

A CHRISTMAS POEM

It's Christmas Eve
What's that noise?
Could it be Santa
With gifts and toys?
Tired eyes, restless sighs,
Ever changing tiny smiles.
Is that Santa?
Did he call?
Leaving gifts for one and all.

Peter Woolley

CHRISTMAS

The season of Christmas brings joy to life,
It is the time when the world celebrates the birth of Christ.
The rich and the wealthy put good gifts together,
The poor and the needy receive heart-warming desires.

The season of Christmas brings goodwill to men,
It inspires and uplifts the lives of children.
It appeals to families far and near,
It helps to unite people everywhere.

The season of Christmas is special to me,
In it I find joy and superb beauty.
It helps to suppress my doubts and my fears,
And I am truly delighted when Christmas is here.

Julliet Miller

GIVING

Presents sit sheltered under the greenery,
Standing proud amidst sparkling scenery,
Waiting to be opened with relish,
Wrapping no longer trying to embellish.

Time is valued and short,
Shopping trips you cannot abort.
What to buy family or friends?
Gifts that won't make do and mend.

Cards adorn every inch of mantle and wall,
Postie keeps coming to pay a call.
Favourites are put in prominent positions,
Likely to engage seasonal missions.

Philip Housbey

CHRISTMAS

Christmas is drawing near, everyone is so excited and cheerful,
The children are ecstatic, expecting everything,
But they can forget the most priceless gift of all,
It's Mary's baby son, Jesus, who was born in a poor stable,
In a manger for his bed, from St Matthew's Gospel, I have read;
The Salvation Army play their carols and collect for their good deeds,
The churches are welcoming everyone to celebrate the good news.
Receiving Holy Communion, singing carols by candlelight in the pews;
The church bells are soundly pealing,
The mince pies are warming, their aroma is so appealing;
Open your hearts and minds to receive The Holy Trinity,
The one-in-three and the three-in-one,
Since God created His own mysterious divinity;
The Father, the Son, the Holy Spirit,
Since the beginning of the early Christians, who did believe.

Irene Greenan

MIDNIGHT COMMUNION

Once more the infant Christ shall be conceived,
The Saviour of the world received.
As in this mystic hour, when for our sakes
The mantled flesh of men He takes.

We kneel together for the wine and bread,
As silence deepens, love is spread.
Himself He gives, our emptiness to fill,
As feeding in His light we do His will.

Bathed in the nimbus of the Lord of Light
We greet the glory of this Christmas night,
Joining in carols' glad refrains
That the blessing of His birth remains.

Idris Woodfield

A Reason For Christmas

Christmas is a time
For everyone on Earth,
Christmas is a time
To celebrate a birth.

The birth of a child
Who means a great deal,
The birth of a child
Who came to save and heal.

To heal Mankind
And to set him straight,
Before the time comes
When it will be too late.

For Jesus Christ was born
For Mankind's sake,
To stop us all
From making a terrible mistake.

He spread His love
And the word of His Father
To any who would listen
And any who would gather.

So listen all of Mankind
And hear it well,
For Jesus gave His life
For you and me as well.

For He died on the Cross
And then He was arisen,
Raised to His Father
Who was in Heaven.

Then sent back to Earth,
To tell us all
God He has forgiven
God is all.

John Morris

CHRISTMAS

Christmas is coming, the reindeers are getting fat
Father Christmas took. I've left him a chunky KitKat
Oh please get here soon, I really can hardly wait
It's the 24th of December already; oh Mummy is he late?

I've done my jobs; bought presents, decorated the tree
Written my letter to Father Christmas; not one page but 23!
Helped Mummy make mince pies and iced the Christmas cake
Is it time yet Mummy? Is he here? Where is he for goodness sake?

It must be time now surely? Oh! Perhaps he's passed me by
I've been a good girl. Honest. Well, I've really tried
Oh, what's that noise? That pitter-patter sound upon the roof?
Oh if I'm not mistaken it's the sound of a reindeer hoof.

Must close my eyes, go to sleep. Can't let him find me peeping
I know Father Christmas only visits when we are all a-sleeping
I only hope and pray he remembers my puppy, cat and horse
And please don't forget Daddy, I think he wants a Porsche!

Michelle Borrett

THE CHILD OF THE MANGER - YET A KING

The cold, chilled air of night
Crept through rough slats
Of a stable door
Where a newborn child
Laid in a cattle trough
On a bed of straw

A lone star
Shed its dazzling rays
Of piercing light
To welcome the birth
Of a King
On that wondrous night

A tired young mother
Gazed with watchful love
Upon her infant Son
The Word made Flesh
His earthly pilgrimage
Had just begun

Light of the world
You came -
To banish all darkness
Suffering and pain
You opened the window of Heaven
Bearing our sorrow and shame

Here we touch the Infinite
Mystical union
Betwixt God and Man
Inexhaustible love
That changed the world
Since it first began

Born in poverty
A refugee to be
Born a King
To save a child
Like you and me

The Child of the manger - yet a King

Frances M Gorton

IT COMES EVERY YEAR

It comes unexpected, when I forget
that I resent all the warnings
and things to be done.

Every year, to those who know
to be open in heart, the lights go on,
that blessed time again.

Something in me doesn't want
to be so obvious, yet I get stopped,
half prepared.

With a week to go, I can't get away
from the magic and the little things
that make me feel small.

Mostly, it comes too early
and not on the 25th,
but when it feels like it.

Michael Hutchinson

WHEN CAMELS BLINKED

While holding heads high with looks of disdain,
Some camels stared down into a cowshed.
Little they cared about King Herod's reign.
They wondered about their Magi instead.
When their Three Wise Men had talked to that King
From their camel-loads they'd offered him - *nothing!*

But soon had left to follow their bright star
Which took them from a palace to an inn.
Crowded out with people from near and far,
Not even Magi could they now squeeze in.
Luckily the night sky spilled with starlight
Which - camels blinked - was filled with
Winged angels bright.

Surely they dreamed? Then they see with surprise
That inside the cowshed, instead of food,
Most carefully wrapped, a baby lies
In the manger near which its parents stood . . .
Why are oxen on their knees round this bed?
Why are their own Three Wise Men so - excited?

Angel song mixes with cattle lowing,
The mother takes the baby in her arms.
Overhead, the Magi Star is glowing.
The Wise Men warn the parents of those harms
Herod intends for all the newly born.
Then three gifts they take down from bales
Camel borne.

The camels join oxen down on their knees,
Overcome by sudden feeling
That they also, the Holy Babe should please.
Like their own three Magi kneeling
To give gold, frankincense and myrrh, morning
Saw camels stalk off, that shed no longer scorning.

C C

CHRISTMAS JOURNEY

Mirrored o'er the face of time, each
Christmas a new milestone,
a place to rest from busy lives,
in the peace and warmth of home.

The shining star waits overhead,
to guide us to the manger,
that tiny babe, the *line of faith*
is sheltered from all danger.

Sometimes trials allotted,
are oft' too heavy a load
a donkey is patiently waiting
with a love that forever efolds.

Follow this path to the manger,
encompass each moment of gold,
welcome this promised redeemer
God's gift by prophets foretold.

Olive Bedford

THE LORD'S BIRTHDAY

When I look around the table
With my family gathered here
I know this day of Christmas
Is my favourite of the year
For often we are parted
And scattered far and wide
But on the good Lord's birthday
I have you at my side
Of course we all had troubles
When the year seemed dark and long
But on this special time of Christmas
We unite and faith is strong
And to see your happy faces
Fills my heart with joy and love
For I know the Saviour Jesus
Watches o'er us from above.

June Davies

I'VE SEEN SANTA CLAUS!

'Yes! I've seen Santa Claus,' said Mel.

When I was in the orphanage
He was an old man
He gave me a toy
Yes, he was an old man
With icicles in his whiskers
The ramblings of a brain-damaged mind?
He took a swig of his tea
To laughter and chuckles
As Christmas songs played on the radio
Who knows?

Paul Wilkins

CHRISTMAS - WITHOUT CHRIST?

Why do we have to take the christ out of Christmas?
Implications here are enormous,
My Saviour was born at this time of year,
So why to mention His name should I fear?
Others their own beliefs must follow,
I will not shout and holler,
Father Christmas, by hundreds of children, has been adored,
So why now, has he too, been outlawed?
For some the festivities in September begun,
For others no baubles or mistletoe will be hung,
Individuals must have the choice,
But Christians, no longer seem to have a voice,
For me December is the month to celebrate,
September, too early, January too late.

Nita Roskilly

OUR CHRISTMAS SONNET 2004

Our warm home is a real joy to behold,
Our Christmas tree is small, but with good cheer,
Decorations, cards, from friends new and old,
Baubles and all, they come out ev'ry year.
With family and friends, we have enough,
So good food, wine and gifts, let us then share,
The lonely, the sad and sick find it tough,
We took hampers to ill folk, bringing cheer.
At Midnight Mass, the faithful sang with love,
'True peace be with all men,' said in loud voice,
Carols, choir and incense praise the Above,
Good tidings we bring, so let us rejoice.
I was ill with cancer two years ago,
Now married and healthy, I love life so.

Mary May Robertson

A QUIET TRUE CHRISTMAS

It's quite a long time ago,
I mean a long time ago in Bethlehem
When somebody quite distinct was born to
Suffer for us, that we may live.

It's quite long before now when Messiah
Was born in a manger, wrapped with
Swaddling cloths, visited by the shepherds
Guarded by a lone star, presented with three gifts
He laid down His life for the sins of all.

He wished to die, that we may live.
He chose to suffer, so that we can have
Eternal life in abundance, He agreed to be
Tormented so that we can be saved,
What a wonderful man of long time ago,
Who still lives with us for ever more.

He shed His blood for people's sake,
He was buried, yet He arose again,
Our beloved Saviour all the time,
The first living among the dead,
Jesus, Emmanuel, son of David.

The Lion of the tribe of Judah
What a quiet, distinct man, You are!
Because You died, because You rose
Because You live, You surrender, Your life for us to live.

With this we can see tomorrow and have eternal life,
For the sting of death has no power over us again.
What a quiet, true Christmas You gave us
To remember the day, a Saviour was given to us.

Though many do not believe that You have come
For some are still expecting You to come while
Others are anxious to see Your second coming
A day believes the world will be at rest.

Adegoke Austin Adedamola

STAR OF BETHLEHEM

A star of Bethlehem shines so bright,
Over a stable, it shines tonight,
For on this special Christmas morn,
The son of God, Lord Jesus was born.

It guided shepherds and wise men three,
To the place where the dear child lay,
The archangels sang for joy,
At the birth of this little boy.

The stable was so old and dank,
The three wise men to their knees they sank.
Gold, frankincense and myrrh were the gifts they brought,
They travelled from far away to see this special child sought.

Ox and ass and lambs kept warm,
The new baby that had just been born,
Wrapped in swaddling clothes in a manger lay,
Born upon a special Christmas Day.

Barbara Holme

CHRISTMAS JOY

First came the shepherds to the stable throne
Who forgetting their peasant thrift
In spontaneous adoration, offered a gift,
Each shepherd He cherished as His own.

Kings travelled long, knew many a weary hour,
Camels were dear, they ignored the cost,
A view of that star must not be lost:
At last an infant, helpless, innocent of power.

Intuitively, they know they are in the Divine Presence,
And with kingly adoration, offer their rich presents.

The great heart receives first the lowly, then the peer,
His lifestyle showed the state He preferred,
Mankind at last with simplicity is stirred,
When love is perfected, His Kingdom will be near.

Mary Frances Mooney

CHRISTMAS APPROACHES LIKE A WAVE

Standing on glittered sand in moonless night,
Hanging baubles in the shifting sky, as
Earth creaks clockwise on the heaviest spring
And salt black sea breathes in, and up and up
And waves too high to save the numbered stars,
Bulb bright, but hanging dusty in the dark.
Time is strange with sea so high
And looking through a castle wall of glass
See Christmas form (and wish with all your might
That this year love will come at last, and last)
Breaking on the glitter sanded moonless night.

Susan Wren

THE ESSENCE OF CHRISTMAS

Oh where is the essence
Where did it go?
The essence of Christmas
I used to know
Children and laughter
Holly and mistletoe
Wrapping up parcels
With ribbons and bow
Where is the essence
Of dumplings and cake
Steak pie and roast
In the oven to bake?
Listening for Santa
And hearing sleigh bells
Oh bring back the Christmas
That I used to know.

Opal Innsbruk

CHRISTMAS (CREDIT) CARDS

Christmas came and went again
It left me very poor
My credit cards were hammered
The wolves are at the door.

I have to spend a fortune
Tradition says I should
I'm sure I'll pay the cards off soon
I only wish I could!

Stein Dunne

CHRISTMAS

A tinsel fairy looks down on a child
Innocence absorbed beneath a pining tree
Painted briefly on a face, the jingle song of glee
Absorbs the tactile wrapping of love's fare
And stares into the gentle eyes of care

And in the distant, church bells musty gong
Lie scented halls of candle wax and song
Alive with distant echoes of a spirit here yet gone
And all the grown-up children sit and stare
And look into the eyes of love and care

And did these children flocking to a light
Hope to regain this inner Christmas sight?
And once again to feel themselves alone
Absorbed in such a purity of tone
In the stable, ever-loving warmth of home.

Brin Parsons

CHRISTMAS WISH

I'd like a matching pair
Of kind thoughts and deeds;
The starlight of respect
To feed dignity's needs;
Twinkling smiles and words,
Parcels of your time
The spirit of Christmas
In this world of mime.

Anita Layland

BEFORE CHRISTMAS SHOULD LEAVE US

Before our Christmas should leave us in dizzy secular quests
Time to remember, it was the lost, Bethlehem babe came to save
How that holy child calls us to real fulfilment of love and purpose
His Father's kingdom motivates our lives to peace and brotherhood
So man's fears *to be or not to be*, shall move away from centre stage.

The spring to come? See already that stable Christ-child's smile
Seek now that joy, happiness and love unfailing - God so wanted for us
Beautiful springboard of truth and hope - dissolving dark horizons
His caring grace - to edge us back to creative paths of light
The planets' creator designed for us to be the best that we can be.

Watch keenly stars that fall and those that brightly shine before us
For this time surely - three wise men - could never be enough
Walk reverently this shorter journey - 'til Christ shall come again
When those angels herald him - and sing once more of glory
What will mankind - be able to offer - to Him -
Then?

Don Harris

THE SECRET CHRISTMAS PRESENT

Dear Santa, please may I have a dolly,
And I just think I'll call it Polly.
But please Santa make it snow,
Because I would really like to throw
A snowball at my daddy
And then return to my mammy.
Oh and I've just forgot,
There is something else
That I've not got,
But unfortunately I cannot tell what,
Because it's not to be known too well.

Camille Gillon (7)

A Winter's Imprint

The air is so rich with this cleaning tool
Which states, 'Out with the old and in with the new'!
Were the air to be coloured, it would be frosty blue
Showing the true festive spirit now in full view.
Branches now sag under the heavy white snow,
A robin digs and looks for the red berries below.

Like jewels, icicles hang from the trees,
Crisp ice crackles from under the snow and the leaves.
Early morning smoke from a lone chimney-pot blows -
Reflecting the warmth as the inner-hearth glows.
Tree lights adorn windows as the dawn chorus alights,
Frost paints ornate patterns upon the windows now bright.

Trees are stripped naked with no valour or vice,
A few bronze leaves remain, now stiff with the ice.
Meadows turn into golden seas as the countryside slows,
Hares run freely and pheasants fly with the crows.
Foot trodden imprints embellish the snow,
Imprints of all kinds does Mother Nature show.

Darryl Benson

Deep Meaning

Christmas time means to me
The family and a Christmas tree
Of peace on Earth, goodwill to men
A baby to die and rise again
A world where people live together
And all unite for ever and ever.

Shirley Parker

CRACKERS ABOUT CHRISTMAS

When evenings are darker
And winter is here -
We make ourselves cosy indoors
And look forward to Christmas cheer.

It's not the weather for salad
Dear Mum, we want suet pud -
And tho' we're not very naughty
We try to be extra good.

It's crackers and carols for Christmas
And gifts for the people you love -
Stockings pinned up at the chimney
And blessings poured down from above.

Penny Miller

THE CHRISTMAS I FORGOT

It is the time we go out and spend lots of dosh
While children stuff their faces with masses of tosh.
My spending is at an all time high,
So what! I can take a loan right up to the sky.
The crates are stacked by the back door,
Better than any fridge for sure.
The booze is flowing, the parties begun,
Music is banging and we are having fun.
At the end of the session I climb into bed
And pictures of the day go through my head.
Have I forgot something! Oh what can it be?
I looked at the crib and it came back to me.

Ann Wood

Phenomenon

The world is waiting in stillness, under a bright, starry sky.
The whole of nature is silent, at the wondrous event which draws nigh.

Imagine these fields at the first time,
Back down those two thousand years,
When all of the creatures, in reverence,
Stopped, and forgot all their fears.

A bright star sped through the heavens,
Then rested in one special place,
At which every single field animal
Was surprised, and raised up its face.

Each one knew something was happening,
Over which there was no control.
Rabbit sat by fox, and rat stood by mouse,
To be joined by the stoat and the vole.

'Look at this,' said the shrew to the hedgehog.
'Have you ever seen a star shine so bright?'
'Not in my lifetime,' he answered,
'But this is a phenomenal night.'

The birds drifted down from the treetops.
The owls and the bats stopped their noise.
Row upon row of furry beings
Were united, in one unique voice.

'This is the birth of Lord Jesus,
The one of whom we were told,
And the Wise Men are taking him presents,
Of frankincense, myrrh and of gold.'

Across the whole world spread the whisper,
Among creatures both large and small,
That God's Son was born in a stable,
Who came to give love to us all.

Now in the fields they are gathering, as they did on that night long ago,
To lift up their eyes to The Bright Star, announcing The Birth,
With its glow.

Lorna Lea

THE STAR

It
happened
many years ago,
so often has been
told, the miracle of Jesus'
birth at Christmas long ago. The
Star hung over Bethlehem, where in a
manger lay the baby boy child Jesus Christ,
born on Christmas Day. People came from far and wide
Wise Men and shepherds too, and angels and the Heavenly Host praised
God amidst the snow. They came and knelt, and bowed their
heads, beside the crib to see, Mary's tiny miracle,
this wondrous Deity. And that is why at
Christmas time we celebrate
His birth, as church bells
ring and choirs sing
joy and peace
to all on
Earth.

Pauline Phillips

PRAYER FOR CHRISTMAS - THE GIFT OF HOPE

The greatest gift anyone can give another person is hope.
Hope creates the desire to live and to become well,
To overcome all adversity and to fight against the odds.
Hope builds on hope and gives a reason to survive.

The birth of a baby brings hope for the future to all of us.
We have a new life and a new beginning.
Lord, through the birth of the baby Jesus
We become filled with hope and promise.

Hope is the greatest gift one human being can give another.

Lord, help us to give each other the gift of hope
Now and always,
Amen.

Maria Dabrowska

CHRISTMAS IN THE DESERT

Her landscape is a barren field, ravages of war,
Holding up a dirty bowl with eyes that plead for more,
She doesn't understand why peace does not come soon,
Squatting on the filthy floor, beneath a ravaged moon,
Santa does not visit this broken war-torn land,
Military soldiers stand with their gun to hand,
Think of all the children starving in the world,
Neighbour fighting neighbour - hatred there unfurls,
Her little naked body, flies upon her eyes,
Holding hands together they look towards the skies,
Maybe food will come - across from foreign lands,
Christmas in the desert spent starving in the sands.

Winifred Curran

DANNI'S CHRISTMAS

Christmas carols go round and round,
Sleigh bells ring, they make a nice sound.
Lots of people are happy today,
So they can go out to play.
They throw some snow,
Until it's time to go,
Then they get in and have a nice drink,
Then they put their pyjamas on that are so pink.

Lots of people put up their tree,
We can sit around our tree, to have a nice cup of tea.
The decorations are so bright; it's a shame when we have to
                                                take them down,
But at least you do have your gown.

Danni Render (5)

CHRISTMAS

Christmas is a magic time,
Full of warmth, joy and good cheer,
The birth of Christ our Saviour,
In all our hearts is dear.
He was born in a stable
And died on the cross.
Our souls he saved
And we felt the loss.
Hope all of these things
And many more too,
Make this Christmas special,
The best yet for you.

J Sayner

THE GREATEST GIFT

Christmas, the season of gifts giving,
Time for gifts of love and more, on the move here, there
                                              and everywhere
Love without explanation?
What would you like for Christmas?
You might have an endless list . . .
Christmas filled with loads of gifts paid or prayed for!

Looking forward to the Christmas hats, cards, decorations,
Looking forward to *being* Santa Claus,
Looking forward to the turkey, cakes, chocolates - probably some
Quality Street and Ferrero Rocher, endless things to eat . . .
Loads of goodies the eyes to meet . . .
Looking forward to reaching out to your gifts on the nicely
                                            decorated Christmas tree . . .
Looking forward to Jesus Christ, the greatest gift someday . . .

Tola Ajala

CHRISTMAS CAME EARLY
(For Ash)

Dewdrop lips and enchanting green eyes
Come Christmas Day Santa can keep his surprise
For mine came early and cannot be topped;
I do not need a gift, I've already got the lot.

She sparkles, she glitters, she brightens up my life
So forgot the tree, the snow, the lights . . .

For this Christmas I'm not dreaming of what Bing did
This Christmas will be special, because of what she already gives.

Ian Duncan

NEARLY TWENTY-FIVE

Dear Santa,
This year I don't want socks,
I would prefer an Xbox,
I know I'm almost twenty-five,
but the kid in me is still alive.

The aftershave that I'm expecting,
the turkey that I'll be dissecting,
are not as fun as games and toys,
that you'll be bringing little boys.

So Santa when you come to me
and place my gifts under the tree,
just remember the kid inside
and forget I'm nearly twenty-five.

Michael Gavin

SNOWFLAKES

Snowflakes spinning
Carols singing
Shining lights
Snowball fights
Wine and cheers
Santa's reindeers
A pretty Christmas tree
Christmas pudding
For you and me
The snow is deep
Santa's coming
So get to sleep.

Eliza Hickinson

CHRISTMAS SONNET

When Christmas comes around again each year
And people turn their thoughts to love and peace,
When shoppers buy their turkey and their geese
And Christmas music rings out loud and clear;
As revellers lay in extra food and beer
And children's laughter sounds on winter air,
Then is the time when all should stop and spare
A thought for those who cannot, will not, hear
The message that should reign in all our homes:
That everyone, no matter where he roams,
Should learn to live in peace and without strife,
To think of every single man as brother,
To live with love and not to hurt another.
This is the secret of a better life.

Judith Hinds

THE FLIPPANT HOUSEWIFE

The twenty-fifth arrives . . .
Skateboards skim along the drives;
All the children's presents, all the food and all the wine,
It's oh so great to be living in this busy modern time,
And Father Christmas has been so generous,
No one would ever guess
That his reindeer couldn't make it quite as far as Bangladesh:
Oh well, maybe next year!

Beryl Messham

A Christmas Wish

May the magic hours of Christmas,
Be with you all the year,
Happy family meetings,
That brings us Christmas cheer,
May it bring us all together,
Reunited for a while,
Forgetting all their troubles,
That vanish with a smile,
The holly and the mistletoe,
The joy that we all share,
The loving and the giving,
To know that people care,
When it is all over,
May our friendship still remain,
With happy Christmas memories,
Till Christmas comes again.

Vera Parsonage

THE GLORY OF CHRISTMAS

Christmas's enchantment arrives
with ribbons of red or dark green.
The Christmas tree brightens our house;
its blinking lights flashing inside.

A soulful loud laugh of, 'Ho! Ho!'
sends Santa's round belly swaying.
Kids hurry to climb on his lap
to tell him of all their wishes.

The candles blaze forth in a church,
and flickering rays cut the darkness.
The twinkling stars shine through panes,
as images on a mirror.

The choristers sing like angels;
their ethereal voices soar.
They praise our God for the Savior,
as heavenly hosts from above.

Patricia Cruzan

CHRISTMAS TREE

Happy, cheerful faces
Full of Christmas glee
Eyes wide open in excitement
As we choose our Christmas tree

Laughter and giggles echo
As we get it in the car
Will we ever get home with it
Or have we gone a foot too far?

Finally we get there
And the tree takes pride of place
Decorated with lights and tinsel
And an angel dressed in lace

I wish I could catch this moment
Keep it with me for when times seem glum
The excitement of my children
One proud and happy mum

Karen Giles

THE INVISIBLE LOVE

The leafless trees and longest ever shadows;
The shortest days and coldest ever nights
All tell us season winter's here
To keep us company.

The brightest lights and lowest ever sunshine;
The grey-breathed days with tingling nose and toes
Remind us of the autumn gone
And springtime yet to come.

The days are short, but not the depth of feeling
With which we celebrate the baby's birth.
A wondrous time; we should be glad:
The Saviour's come again!

Enjoy the joyful strains and words of Christmas;
Rejoice with men of peace who wish you well.
Accept the gift December brings:
The love; invisible love.

Frank L Appleyard

MADONNA AND CHILD

I don't know what it's like 'to be with child',
To sense his presence long before there's any evidence,
To feel her move and be her sustenance
Until that day when life breaks forth
And after all the agony the child is there for all to see
So that which shapes their destiny begins its influence.
Mary knew, as in her arms she held that Precious One,
Her firstborn son,
Remembering, no doubt, the day it all began,
A visitation from a strange, angelic man
Who told her it was no one less than God Himself
Who'd plant the seed and prosper her obedience.
God is with us, knowing all the ins and outs of our existence,
Vulnerable, and yet remaining over all,
His sleeves rolled up in readiness to clear aside the human mess,
And, having once been born, to bear the necessary pain
In order that His people might be born again.

Bob White

WINTER PICTURE

I look at a picture of winter
I see blankets of snow beside a river of ice
Children skate along holding lanterns so bright

I can hear the laughter and feel the cold
The frozen stream clings to my feet
Snow melts on my palm, surrendering to the heat

My picture isn't perfect, it doesn't portray love
I see myself alone and my picture is empty
Only to be complete once you are with me

Taking my hand you soothe away the cold
The warmth of your skin calms the chill
We stand in my picture embracing firm and still

My cold, winter picture glows with the strength of love
An added magic to the Christmas scene
A perfect picture mirrored only in my dream . . .

Beverley Morton

A Jolly Holly Christmas

We were together at Christmas
yet I could have been on my own.
With your stern faced body language,
I've never felt so alone.

Have a merry, merry Christmas
I hear the choirs sing.
A song of joy and peace and love
is the message that they bring.

We were together at Christmas.
Together but not a pair.
Your coldness overwhelmed my anguish.
I could have been anywhere.

Oh have a jolly, holly Christmas
with a shining, fairy-lit tree.
With peace and love, goodwill to men
but not for me.

Maureen Reynolds

COME TO BETHLEHEM

Come all of you to Bethlehem,
Come see the baby boy,
Born this day in Bethlehem
To bring us peace and joy.

Hurry to the stable bare,
You shepherds of the field,
Bring your fleece and woolly sheep,
Give Him your finest yield.

Who's this I see, come to the door,
In robes of silk and gold?
Three Wise Men with precious gifts,
So wondrous to behold.

They all bow down to the tiny babe,
In a stable cold and dark,
As angels fill the sky with song
And bid the people hark.

Patricia Adele Draper

GETTING READY FOR CHRISTMAS

It certainly isn't hard to remember,
That today is the first of December.
Christmas time is almost upon us,
How I hate all the bother and fuss.

Everyone's busy with presents to buy,
Christmas cards and toys, my, oh my.
Extra food to cook, freeze and store,
Money's all gone can't buy any more.

Queue up to post parcels on their way,
As most of my friends live far away.
Concerts, parties and eating out,
All that rich food brings on my gout.

Church services and carol singing,
Midnight mass with church bells ringing.
Wishing everyone a merry Christmas.
Christmas Day with family, what bliss.

Rosemary Davies

LITTLE INFANT'S TIME

It's snowing while wind is draining trees,
smoke is bursting from chimneys while children
are decorating Christmas trees.
The whole family is devoting themselves to the event,
everyone smiles and promises to be good to each other.
Adults are turning into kids and remember
the tenderness of infancy.
The reunion time.

Silent night, Holy night,
the moonlight is on, everything is bright.
After a while, family meets again
at this event, where winter falls like rain.
Joy and smiles around the table
in every home, the atmosphere is enjoyable.
I remember this memorable time
everytime I feel I've crossed the red line.
Then my sorrow's gone,
I know I'll end this year happy once again.

Joyan Jomond

CHRISTMAS PRESENT BUS STOP

I knew what we were doing
When we papered the bus stop.
The crisp cellophane slipped
From the coloured Christmas rolls,
And we began our night's work.
Unrolling sheaf after sheaf.
Slipping the womb of Christmas
Colour, around the stand.
The unmistakable rip of Sellotape
Gluing the laminate in place.
With loving kindness
We enveloped the whole stand.
Top to bottom.
And standing back,
The dawn chorus breaking,
We admired our work.
Our very own Christmas present
Bus stop.

Daniel Brendan Courtney

CHRISTMAS LAUGHTER

Well, here it is again my friends, at the end of another year
Just in time is Christmas with its pleasures and good cheer
The Christmas tree, the crackers and the tasty food to eat
The family round and the beautiful sound of carols sung so sweet

And tell me once again Nan, how you all made paper chains
To hang up to the ceiling, where you hoped they would remain
And how you hung up stockings so late on Christmas night
And woke at dawn to feel for all the goodies stuffed inside

That's how we remember Christmas of the past
How lovely to imagine that those old days could last
For some they have, in spirit, but other folk will know
That now it comes with frozen food and pretty plastic snow

No dash to get the turkey - just store it in the freezer
Defrost it with the other food while Mother takes a breather
The children watch their videos and play computer games
Yet now, like then, the house still rings with laughter just the same.

Norma Griffiths

WHAT IS CHRISTMAS?

Christmas is fairy lights on the tree,
Christmas is cards, to you, from me,
Christmas is Santa with his sack,
Christmas is gifts to wrap and pack,
Christmas is turkey, mince pies and wine,
Christmas is having the family to dine.
Christmas is lots of presents and toys,
Christmas is for good girls and boys,
Christmas is for people, for everyone,
Christmas is God's only beloved son.
Christmas is God's wonderful gift to us,
Christmas is the precious Lord Jesus,
Christmas is a stable, cold and bare,
Christmas is the shepherds, kneeling there,
Christmas is the bright shining star,
Christmas is the wise men from afar,
Christmas is God's grace and love divine,
Christmas is Jesus, He is yours and mine.

Joan Williams

BETHLEHEM

When the herd was watching
In the midnight chill
Came a spotless lambkin
From the heavenly hill.

Snow was on the mountains
And the wind was cold
And from God's own garden
Dropped a rose of gold.

When 'twas a bitter winter
Houseless and forlorn
In a starlit stable
Christ the babe was born.

Welcome heavenly lambkin
Welcome golden rose
Alleluia baby
Wrapped in swaddling clothes.

D A Sheasby

CHRISTMAS WHISPERS

Another year of missing you.
Somehow it hasn't flown.
Every day you cross my thoughts.
How are you? How much have you grown?

And I wonder what things you like to do . . .
Are you doing well in school?
Do you still like to draw those funny cars?
Are the goodies still the baddies? Or did you change the rules?

But today I simply wonder,
Do you ever think of me?
Do I cross your mind at Christmas time?
Or any other special day?

Do you feel the weight of another year?
Is there understanding in one so young?
Do you whisper, *'I love you daddy.'*
When I whisper, *'I love you my son.'*

Paul Barrington

TAKE A BREAK

The parties are over, the people are gone;
We gaze in dismay at the work to be done.
So let's get away from the tinsel and tree,
And take a brisk walk down by the sea.

There's the fridge to sort out and letters to write.
'Please just take a break. Will you come? Yes, that's right!'
'Forget for a moment, the tinsel and tree
The paper and cards and come out with me.'

It's freezing out here yet the sea is so blue,
The sun is a-shining, welcoming you.
The silver white breakers roll gently ashore.
Can you feel tension easing? Can you feel peace once more?

Just a few precious moments away from the chores
To the peace that is Christmas, down by the shore
Refreshed once again, homeward we'll go
There's work to be done but our hearts are aglow.

Barbara Dunning

Christmas Can Be Lonely

The old man wanders down the street, his ancient dog in tow
Houses spill their Christmas lights, their windows all aglow.
Sounds of laughter fill the air as families dine together
Warm and cosy in their homes, safe from wintry weather.
The man wears only threadbare clothes and feels chilled to the bone
But better out here in the streets than sitting home alone.
His faithful dog is all he has, his best and only friend
He knows their friendship will endure right up to the end.
Sometimes people hurry past and overtake the pair
No one seems to spare a glance and no one seems to care.
The old man thinks of childhood days when Christmas was a joy
When everything was magic to the eyes of a small boy.
The world had seemed so wonderful, the future oh so bright
But now he knows each lonely day leads to a lonely night.
Those of us with families and friends who number many
Should say a prayer at Christmas time for folk who have not any.
And when we sit before the fire and watch each blazing log
Spare a thought for lonely souls like the old man and his dog.

Denise Castellani

THOUGHTS OF CHRISTMAS

Christmas time, lots of tinsel
Mulled wine, apple schnitzel
Too much food, ready to burst
Too much drink, a terrible thirst

Parcels wrapped with shiny bows
Rudolf with his big red nose
Christmas candles to be lighted
Not going to bed, too excited

The lights upon the fir tree
Bring memories to mind for me to see
Santa Claus with robes of red
Stockings hung, it's time for bed

Children's faces alight with glee
For parents it's a joy to see
Peace on Earth, goodwill to all
I can't wait for Christmas to call.

Gail Wooton

A Christmas Thought

Tomorrow will be Christmas Day,
When we open presents and watch children play;
But don't forget what Christmas means,
When God above did Heaven leave.

To Earth He came in human form,
Born of a virgin so humble and forlorn;
To Earth He came, our people to save,
The baby Jesus was His name.

So Christmas is a time for joy,
But spare a thought for that small boy;
He healed the sick, made the blind see,
From leprosy He did not flee.

He did not sin, He was a good man,
But from the start He knew God's plan;
He had to die upon the Cross
Our souls to save, oh what a loss.

Thelma Cook

WINTER WARMS THE SOUL WITHIN ME

Church bells chime in a darker clime
when winter sets her tears upon me.
Storms that blow with ice and snow
make birds migrate to a fairer state,
chirping happily as they go.

But Christmas time is a radiant time
and winter shines her light upon me
with joyous bells and a fairy tale,
hearts all aglow with mistletoe
whilst peace prevails on hill and dale.

Poetic lines are nursery rhymes
when winter sets her calm upon me,
and the glory of the wondrous story
tells of Bethlehem - so holy, holy.
Weeping tears no longer haunt me
for winter warms the soul within me.

Joyce Hemsley

FESTIVE SPIRITS
(Written for Natasha Lee)

Crisp may be the wintry crest
A snowy white blanket,
Over which love may rest
Where Mother Nature may be the gentler queen
Beneath the sheet, where her love's not seen;
Kissed so pleasantly, sweet upon soil
Deeper is love when such love is so royal;
Endlessly whispered like an eternal chant
In lace and silk of pinks and creams
Angelic blues and red that screams;
Just for season's choice of bliss
With mistletoe and a heart to kiss
The wood hearth burning to spirit occasion
For the flavours of a turkey roast
Sweet honey, lemon and cranberry dressing
Embellished with chestnuts, fired and warm
It is the season when the soul is born
And humanity lends a kinder ear
So a Happy Christmas and a Happy New Year.

Don Capo

THAT CHRISTMAS GIFT

I am round and slim, a lovely shape
I am a roll of Sellotape
I just go round and round
Many a parcel I have bound

I'm a sheet of Christmas paper
Covered in robins, such a caper
I'm no use unless I can wrap
So where's the gift I'll trap

Here I am a flask of scent
I must be covered and not bent
To a friend I will be sent
In Sellotape and paper, just like a tent

A united trio to make a gift
God gave at Christmas such a lift
Let us remember that stable day
Rejoice again in every way.

Erica Menzies

CHRISTMAS EVE

Locking my door upon
Colours and brightness
Into a night I stepped
Pure in its whiteness.

Moonlight, Orion light
Silvered the meadows,
Trees cast on snowy ground
Wispy blue shadows.

Frost lit by moonshafts lay
Softly a-shimmer,
Hillsides in starlight slept
Palely a-glimmer.

Here where in Heaven-light
Snowfields were gleaming,
More than in tinselled rooms
Christmas had meaning.

Emma Kay

NEW YEAR

And so it starts.

The new year draws near
will it be a time of cheer?

Can we forget the past
and this year just have a blast?

New friends and old
gather around in the cold.

Glasses over flowing
the past tears, not now showing.

And as the clock strikes the tune
happy new year fills the room.

So raise your glass
you're top of the class.

Happy new year my friends
may our friendships never end.

Sarah-Jane Clark

HAPPY CHRISTMAS

Christmas time is here again,
I remember it last year, oh the pain.
First there's the brainpower, what can I buy?
Whatever I get they probably won't like.
Then there's the cash to buy the stuff,
I've saved all year but there's never enough.

Then there's the shopping for all the food
So when they come you can stuff your brood,
And oh what about the Christmas cheer,
'It'll soon be Christmas,' rings in my ear.
Down in the town they're all trimmed up,
The same carols are playing in every shop.

And when the day comes and we've opened out gifts,
To feed the hoard you work double shifts.
You eat and you drink all to excess,
Then suddenly it's over and you're broke and depressed.
But cheer up quick or you might go insane
Because it'll soon be that time of year again.

Margaret Mansbridge

CELEBRATING CHRISTMAS
(Can be sung to the tune 'Once In Royal David's City')

Christmas is a celebration,
It's a time of praise and love,
For the precious, infant Saviour
Came to us from Heaven above.
Jesus Christ, your Lord and mine
Born for us, of David's line.

Christmas is a celebration,
Love came down for one and all;
And as Mary cared for Jesus
In that lowly cattle stall
Shepherds came their gifts to bring,
Angels did their praises sing.

As we share this celebration
On this happy Christmas morn,
Let us thank our Heavenly Father
That His Son, the Christ was born.
Jesus Christ, our King and Lord
Does to all His love afford.

Anne Gray

COLD CHRISTMAS

It's a cold, cold Christmas on the streets,
Under the arches a young girl weeps,
All her dreams have vanished,
Into a world of anguish,
The temperature is minus five,
It will be a miracle if she survives.

Where she comes from, no one cares,
Just another face in a city of fears,
She scrapes a pittance by begging,
If she's clever, she'll get caught robbing,
There is no salvation for this teen child,
Kicked out onto the streets, will she survive?

There's only one road for girls on the street,
But she's not succumbed yet, a master feat,
They taunt her with promises of a better life,
If she gives in, will they treat her alright?
Anyway, the temperature was minus five,
There wasn't a miracle, she didn't survive.

Jane Margaret Isaac

CHRISTMAS EVE

Oh! what a delight
To see the shimmering candlelight
Is it some special occasion
Or is it someone's passion?
It's like Heaven on Earth
God has taken rebirth
Those ringing bells I can hear
To be in my room I can't bear
Let me go, let me enjoy
Let me not be a coy.
That sweet smell of cakes
That my mother never makes
I'm dying to taste all delicacies
That is Christmas specialities
How different is this celebration
A moment of elation
Today I want to touch the sky
To pluck these stars
I want to fly.

Shanu Goyal

CHRISTMAS LONELINESS

I stare at the bottle, just one small drink, all of my troubles into oblivion sink,
But right now I know that I dare not, one drink and my life is shot,
Where is the answer to all of my woe? If only there was some place to go,
To leave all behind me and start again, forget all the worry, the grief and the pain,
It seems I must stay here still, for a time, if only there was someone I could call mine,
Christmas time is worse than the rest, everyone else seems so happy and blessed,
I struggle to cope with everyday chores, longing and longing for just something more,
I've tried all my life to do my best, then when I need help I'm just one of the rest,
I won't take that drink, the struggle is over and I know that one day I'll be in the clover,
With Jesus my friend to care and protect, I'll make it to Heaven to be with Him yet.

J J Saunders

CHRISTMAS IS HERE

Christmas is here
Once a year,
Everyone starts to shout and cheer,
Christmas means joy,
Gifts and toys
For each and every girl and boy.

We all have a laugh and eat some sweets;
Christmas time is full of treats.
As long as we have all been good,
We'll get our gifts as we should,
And if you have been very bad,
Then on Christmas Day you'll be feeling sad.

Jesus was born on this special day,
In a stable He did lay,
Celebration all around,
Lots of noise and a riotous sound.

Everyone had lots of fun,
Singing and laughter for everyone.

Callum Smith

ST PETER'S CHURCH, ON BOXING DAY MORNING

A bottle of Mateus to see me through the day,
Sat upstairs in the loft
While St Peter's church bells play
Sucking on my lumps of coal
Ice cream and lemonade
Complain about the job I do
Whenever I get paid.

While wives pick on their husbands
It's not safe anymore
Everyone's after me
As I crawl above the door.

I finally got hold of the bug
That had been going all around
I creep outside the cupboard
I'm ill and zigzagging down
Vegetable soup for Boxing Day
Stay put in my room through spring
As the wives pick on their men
And Woolton's church bells ring.

Rodger Moir

CHRISTMAS TRUE

Rushing here, rushing there
Christmas, rushing everywhere
Buying this, buying that
Sorry, haven't time to chat.
Twenty more days, shops will shut
Must be something I forgot
Uncle Ted, Auntie Sue
Who else? Oh yes, you.
I've got the turkey, got the ham
Must get that tie for Uncle Sam
All those hours, ready to drop
Must keep going, two days to shop.
Wait, what do they do in a far-off land,
No food, no money, no shops to hand?
Children die for lack of care,
No presents, no tree, no Santa there.
Yet, in their hearts, true Christians they
Through all their hardship to *God* they pray
Christmas, the day when *Jesus* was born,
It's that they celebrate on Christmas morn.

BMF

CHRISTMAS

Not for ourselves - it's for the children.
That's what people say,
buying the tawdry trappings
of a commercialised Christmas Day.

Parents incurring year long debts
to pacify their pampered pets,
overpriced tinsel, toys galore,
presents littering lives and floor.

Better by far to stop and think
of others starving - life on the brink.
No transitory toys in their sad lives,
food, warmth, shelter, their paradise.

Tell your children about the hungry poor,
in far off lands, cold and raw.
Teach them to give, as well as taking,
in the midst of their merry-making.

Spare some thought for those in the world
who long for peace at any price.
Think of the meaning of Christmas time,
love and joy and sacrifice.

Rose Ashwell

CAT CHRISTMAS

Tap, tap
it swings
. . . falls

Gracious pounce
it's caught
. . . then escapes
gets stuck
under the settee

It's alive
I'm watching it
from behind a chair

Can't see me!
swishing tail
ears back
. . . ready - big leap

Caught it, mouse
(silver bubble)

Tired . . . cat nap.

Moira Jean Clelland

JINGLE BOLL*X

With a ho-ho-ho, and away we go,
An' a tra-la-la-la-lal la!

Keep the colds at bay, keep the banshees away,
Let the fires burn, all night and all day,
Let the snow come down on Christmas Day,
To see us merrily on our way.

With a ho-ho-ho, and away we go,
An' a tra-la-la-la-lal la!

With old Rudolph and his red nose,
And Donner and a Blitzen,
Old Santa he'll be grinnin',
Eating mince pies in the kitchen,
And we'll be drinkin' brandy,
Or the odd wee dram o' whisky,
Cos they say one makes you randy,
And the other makes you frisky!

With a ho-ho-ho, and away we go,
An' a tra-la-la-la-lal la!

Paul Andrews

Peace On Earth

Christmas, Christmas all around,
But where can peace on Earth be found?
Not on the Christmas tree
Dressed so beautifully.
Not on the bustling city streets,
Not in Selfridges, Argos or Boots,
Not in the twinkling, colourful lights,
Not in the presents wrapped up tight.
Not in the parties, the food or the drink,
Not even in the children who can't sleep a wink.
But that peace can be found within the heart
Of those who believe the important part,
The Christ of Christmas came to make known,
The love that God has for His own.
The love that sent His only Son
On a mission to die for everyone.
So let the festivities begin,
Rejoice and let Christ in.
After all the party is for His birthday,
For without Him, Christmas is just another day.

Rebecca Walker

CHRISTMAS TIME

I like to think of Christmas as of years ago,
Putting up the holly and the mistletoe.
Children putting up a stocking and decking up a tree,
A cosy log fire burning, to warm the family
This was done on Christmas Eve,
Children were excited about presents Santa would leave!

It is so different in the world of today,
Supermarkets full of goods and different ways to pay.
Food and drink are priority and parties going on,
The last thing on the minds of us, is the coming of God's Son!
We hope His Christmas Spirit be born in us today,
So love, joy and blessed peace be in our hearts, we pray.

May the star that shone over Bethlehem,
Light up our lives as it did then.
So peace can reign in our troubled world now,
That at Christmas we can feel His blessings, somehow!
At this time of our Lord Jesus' birth,
May peace and goodwill towards men, be present on Earth.
The same old Christmas message is still for us to hear,
May the Christmas spirit be with us in the coming year.

Joyce Hallifield

A Christmas Thought

Lord, it's almost Christmas and there is so much to do,
I'm really very busy, and it's all because of you.
There are so many jobs I'm not sure what to do first,
And the crowds of non-Christian shoppers only make things worse.
I must put flowers in the church and decorate the tree,
Change the straw in the manger and set up the nativity.

As well as all the churchy things, there are presents still to buy,
I'm never going to do it all; the hours just seem to fly.
I thought it would help, if I made a list, it took me such an age,
It just goes to show how busy I am; it took a double page!
I've often wondered why Lord, you made Christmas quite so busy,
I get so fraught and stressed; it makes me feels so dizzy!

'Child will you stop, still your busy mind,
Forget about the dos and don'ts, the gifts you've still to find.
Leave the decorations; don't unpack the tree,
Just sit still and in the stillness share this time with me.
Remember those first shepherds; they had no gifts to bring,
And those Wise Men who knelt in the straw before their king.
If you truly want to share this Christmas, and would like to play a part,
Dear child all I ask of you, is the gift of your heart.'

Lynne Cassels

PRESENTS FOR OTHERS

A scarf for cousin Joe, to keep away the chill
A pair of Arsenal football boots for my sister's eldest, Bill
A comfy pair of slippers for Sue who lives in Gwent
And for my niece who lives in Hull, expensive Paris scent.

For cousin Jack who treads the boards, some make-up for his face
And for my auntie up in Perth, fine hankies stitched with lace
My uncle is a music fan, he rocks most every night
And so for him some blue-suede shoes, I think the colour's right.

My brother has a son called Sid, who likes to sow wild flowers
And so for him a spade and trowel to wile away the hours
Auntie Meg is cookery mad, she makes scones by the ton
A sack of currants, flour and eggs will give her hours of fun.

My grandson Nick is boxing mad, the king of sports he loves
A pair of shorts in gold lamé and leather hand-stitched gloves
I have a niece who loves to sing, she drives her parents mad
Some insulation for her walls, I'm sure they will be glad.

Each year it seems to be the same, I shop until I'm vexed
For people who I never see from one year to the next
So this year I've a different plan, on me I will spend well
On chocolates, drink and other fare, and they can go to Hell.

Jennifer Davey

A Fall Of Snow

Another day of shopping, of sore feet, fatigue and stress
no one has the Christmas spirit, most people couldn't care less
with heads bowed down with worry,
they barge and snarl and shove,
spending more than they are earning,
in this season of goodwill and love.
It's been like this for weeks now
and suddenly it's Christmas Eve,
the children are washed and in their beds
at least they still believe.
I yawn and stretch and turn out the light,
peep through the curtains oh! what a sight,
all of the evening without us knowing
the first time in years it started snowing.
It covers the roofs and chimneys and ground
its transformed the night, without making a sound
I hear Christmas carols, and I hum and sway
the weeks of stress seem to fall away.
I hear the sound of a distant church bell
and of friends and neighbours wishing each other well
it's all been worthwhile don't you know,
and all brought on by a fall of snow.

Mike Harrison

CHRISTMAS ALONE

Christmas is a lonely time for most,
All the wishes they have don't come true,
They feel cold and lonely,
Brought about by being alone.

Their loved ones have left them,
Things aren't as they used to be,
They don't bother dressing a tree.

They sit and watch through the window,
As people gaily saunter by,
Yet inside all they want to do is cry.

The meaning of Christmas is not the same,
There are no presents ready wrapped,
To them Christmas is scrapped.

Why? They have lost their soulmate, their best friend,
Christmas used to be for two and now it's only one.

Only the memories they once shared,
For someone they cared.
As today is just another day,
To the rest of us it's Christmas Day.

Carol Paxton

ALONE AT CHRISTMAS

I remember Christmas Eve
From so very long ago;
Of golliwogs and tangerines
Real holly and mistletoe.
Pine-scented logs upon the fire,
The smell of hot mince pies.
Church bells ringing,
Choral singing.
The joy in children's eyes.
Wrapping gifts into the night,
To place beneath the tree.
Tinsel, glitter, fairy lights,
Spelt Christmas out to me.

Now Christmas is spent alone,
There are no gifts, no tree,
No special day.
Just memories,
Held close within.
Alone, with tears a blink away.

Mary Howcroft

REMINISCENCE

Two there were
A man and a lady;
Soon to be three, I thought.

Shelter he asked
For his wife and a baby,
My inn was the last resort.

Tears there were
In the eyes of the lady;
'I've shelter,' I said, 'of a sort.'

Three there were
The man, his wife and the baby
When I went to the stable next morn.

Rumours there were
Of angels and shepherds? Well, maybe!
I treated the story with scorn.

None there are
Now, but in old age I wonder
How fared the young lad that was born?

Muriel Bransdon

OH CHRISTMAS

Every Christmas,
Every Christmas,
I do clearly understand,
Why children sing, those songs of praise,
And gather to celebrate.

Christmas,
Oh Christmas,
I do clearly understand,
The truth in the meaning of God our Lord,
We should all gather, let's celebrate.

Christmas,
Christmas,
I know that you do understand.
It's not all the gifts that you may receive,
It's the thought of giving to people that need.

Christmas,
Oh Christmas,
We all really understand.
It's time for us all to celebrate,
The birth of Jesus Christ.

Emma Jo Taranaski

HOW MUCH FOR CHRISTMAS DAY

Looking back on my life, I have often pondered
On the many, many Christmas Days that I have had to go away.
How my children had spent their Christmas Day, I often wondered
So many times I missed their birthdays and Christmas Day.
The tears in my children's eyes as I left to join a ship
The many letters that I wrote and could not even send.
I would be at sea on Christmas Day, no time to even worship.
None of us had any money, none to borrow, none to lend
Oh what a terrible price we had to pay.
Yet some sold the right to be home on Christmas Day
Some who had the chance to be home, sold that right away.
Would they even think, their children would feel the pain
I wonder how they could do this thing, what would they gain?
Oh what a terrible price to pay
Not to be home on Christmas Day.
Looking back on my life, I try to be brave and hearty
My children will never know the pain I felt in my heart
To have missed their birthday or Christmas party.
Seldom home on Christmas Day, because of my children's need
Yes I have many regrets, but I was away for need not greed.
So many years I have been at sea, how many I cannot say
Nothing can mend my broken heart, away again this Christmas Day.

Francis McGarry

CHRISTMAS DAY

Christmas Day brings happiness and joy
for every girl and every boy,
lots of smiles and lots of laughter
for this year and the year after.

Up goes the tree, all shiny and bright
watch for the star in the deep of the night,
Joseph, Jesus and the Virgin Mary
on top of the tree, we place our fairy.

All the shops buzzing with people
look at the lights on the church and steeple,
shining, twinkling, flashing and bright
watch Santa's sleigh go thro' the night.

Fun and games and party food
to get all folks in the mood,
the young, the old, the white and the black
here comes Santa to empty his sack.

The mistletoe hanging where it can be seen
the children wake and say, 'He's been!'
Down the stairs they go screaming with joy
first the girls and then the young boy.

Jacky Griffiths

CHRISTMAS TIME
(I mean no offence to anyone who doesn't celebrate Christmas)

Mary is at the stable, Jesus is born . . .
people celebrate, from America to Eastbourne!
Cards are given, decorate houses and trees
Hannah has opened her presents, long before three!

What the Dickens is Scrooge up to?
Jumps when all four ghosts go *Boo!*
Tiny Tim happily sings carols
as Bob Cratchit drinks mulled wine straight from the barrels!

It's 25th December, Christmas time . . .
music from Band Aid, Slade, to Cliff's 'Mistletoe And Wine'.
Crackers are pulled, the turkey is eaten . . .
Gillian said, 'There is now snow at Eton!'

Hannah - 'Dad do you want some Smarties?'
'No thanks - I just got over the office parties!'
Later watch repeats of Morecambe & Wise
and The Two Ronnies - shame these never won more prizes!

Jesus, (other gods), Rudolph and Santa . . . see you next year . . .
the twelve days of Christmas are now over, 31st December . . .
said with a tear!

Barry Ryan

CHRISTMAS 2004

Beyond the furthest thistledown wanderings of sidereal dust
Is there perhaps another entity?
Perhaps the entire and unimaginable vastness of our universe
Is held as gently as a child might hold in her cupped hands
The feathered pappus of a dandelion.

Or is creation blind to what it makes
And no more caring than
The swirling, plunging plates on which we drift,
And was Christ speaking merely metaphors
Two thousand years ago,
His Heavenly Father and His Kingdom, dated now,
Projections only of our archetype?

If either be the case:
Whether we ride on camels over shadowed hills
Towards some gracious gesture from beyond the dark,
Or whether we and others like us are the only ones
Who have the chance to spread our slingshot love
Among those sparkling carousels that ride the depths of space,
The path before us is still lit with stars,
Our goal a reconciled and joyful family
Surrounded by the practical and wise.

H A J Fletcher

CHRISTMAS DAY

It's wonderful, is Christmas Day,
For Father Christmas comes - hooray!
But how he gets here we can't say,
Cos we haven't got a chimberly.

Christmas is when Santa brings
All those presents - all those things
That I shall need before the spring.
Ma says it is a great blessing.

You now accept, it's Christmas Day
When everyone gets awful gay,
When lots of goodies come your way,
Have a good time, come what may.

Christmas still has lots to offer
Not much money in the coffer.
It costs as much, one and another
As you get back from friends or mother.

Christmas is expensive, that you'll grant.
Children tell you what they want,
And that adds up - no small amount
And all you get back is a plant!

Walter Dalton

CHRISTMAS IS FOREVER

Ancient of times
Christ the child is born
Sleeping peace
A cry of hope
The world will sing

Morning star
Like heavenly smile
Overpowering beauty
Tears of joy
The world will sing

Light of the world
Everlasting presence
A song among the lilies
Silent and overcoming
The world will sing

Song of songs
Beauty of beauties
Christmas is here
Christmas forever
The world will sing

Vincent Malawo

A Christmas Dilemma

All Christmases are good for trade.
In shops the wares are so displayed
To draw you in. I stop outside.
And wonder should I go inside?

My cards are sent, forgetting none.
I can relax when shopping's done.
So I will buy all presents here.
The window prices are not dear.

For Uncle I will choose a tie.
For Aunt I don't know what to buy.
My cousin may prefer a book,
Or scarf, or gloves. I'll take a look.

I hesitate outside the store
And think of children hungry, poor:
Those orphaned by disease and wars.
For them there is no Santa Claus.

I turn away, the knowledge stings,
So money put aside for things
Like perfumes, scented soaps and socks,
I drop into a charity box.

F G Ward

THEY BELIEVE AGAIN!

They expect gladness.
It is the sad opposite.
Their hearts are broken.
They are destitute.
They do not expect blessings.
They are by themselves.
We make them happy!
They are now optimistic!
They are now fulfilled!
They believe again!
They are enthusiastic!
We bless them with joy!
Songs are being sung!
They are of exaltation!
Everyone is glad!
They mingle with chums!
They are singing melodies!
They are praising Him!
People are content!
We have dispelled broken hearts!
This is wonderful!

Laraine Smith

CHRISTMAS TREE

The tree stands so majestic,
In the daylight.
Then glows with splendour,
Late into the night.
Decorated from head to toe,
With tinsel, baubles and lights.
Presents around the bottom,
Set late in the night.
While children are sleeping,
With their eyes closed tight.
To awaken next morning,
Dash downstairs and see
What Santa has left them,
Squealing with glee.
Presents ripped open in frenzy,
Paper all over the place.
Expensive time I know,
But worth the look on their face.
Then when Christmas is over,
The partying all done.
Back down the tree will go,
To end the Christmas fun.

Anne-Marie Lloyd-Barrett

A Christmas Parable

It was a cold foggy day when the train left the station,
The compartments were full, there was a feeling of elation.
One carriage was very quiet as nobody said a word,
You'd think it wasn't Christmas, it was so absurd.
One lady was knitting bootees, another one was reading,
The third gazed out of the window but the landscape wasn't heeding.
The men were just as solemn, one worked on his laptop,
Another read the paper and the third listened to pop.

The door came partly open and a little child appeared,
He was about two and a half and round the door he peered.
Immediately everything changed and all began to chatter,
The air was filled with noise and fun, what they talked about didn't matter.
Then his anxious mother came, so grateful for their care,
She'd only turned round for a minute and suddenly he wasn't there.

When the little child had gone, they continued to talk rapidly,
For he had lit a fire in them, now they conversed happily.
The baby made a difference to the people on the train,
He brought communication and happiness was their gain.
The baby Jesus brings joy to all of Mankind,
Silence is banished as they their Saviour find.

Rita Hardiman

STARLIGHT

The sky had never been so thick with stars
That blackout night in 1941
How petty seem our earthly wars
Against such magnitude of space.

Singing, we moved along the row
Feeling the dark like a cloak
The sequinned skies above us glow
The Milky Way, a diamond arch.

The lantern beam our only light
For those uncertain of the words
While shepherds watched their flocks by night
O little town of Bethlehem.

Our voices round the rooftops ring
As listeners fill our begging bowl
On Christmas night all Christians sing
God rest ye merry gentlemen.

The sky has never been so thick with stars
Since that Christmas night so long ago.

Marjorie Lloyd

FATHER CHRISTMAS

My brother told me that there wasn't one,
My best friend told me that there wasn't one.
But my mom and dad said that there was one -
I really wanted to believe that there was one,
But I was confused.

I thought about it as long and hard as any six-year-old could,
Then I came to a decision. I was going to write him a letter,
Then I'd know the truth.

I found an old, large brown envelope,
And used my best bright orange lipstick to write with.
Then I put the letter on the end of my bed.
I never told a soul,
Just in case there was any foul play involved.

If the letter was still there the next morning,
It meant that there wasn't one.
If the letter was gone . . .
Then I knew that there was one.
Sadly the letter was still there the next morning,
So there is no Father Christmas!

Angela Kilvert-King

I Remember The Reason

I'm looking through a window, past the twinkling Christmas lights,
And in my mind's eye; I see, that very first Christmas night

There was no Christmas turkey, no Christmas tree with lights,
No shiny gift-wrapped presents, just for my delight

Only a lowly stable, bare and dark and cold,
As I remember that story, the prophets had foretold

When the only present given, was a Son from God above,
And two very special people were blessed by the Father's love

To bring into a heathen world, a Son so pure and true,
That walked upon this very Earth, and died for me and you

I looked past all the glitter; I looked past all the gold,
To remember the birth of our Lord, as the Nativity did unfold

I thank You God for sending, Your Son and special heir,
To save poor lowly sinners, from iniquity and despair

I praise You Almighty Father, for Your gift so precious and great,
As I remember the reason, why this season, we celebrate.

Nigel Lloyd Maltby

A Family Christmas

Presents round the Christmas tree,
Mince pies and turkey roast,
Sweets and jelly with ice cream,
Are things we like the most.

Santa's brought our dog a treat,
A great big juicy bone,
Our cat sat on the holly,
She's sulking all alone.

Grandma can't wash up this year
She is our honoured guest,
Ninety-nine years old last week,
Mum says she needs the rest.

Grandad plays the drums again,
He's only ninety-four,
He's Grandma's little toy boy,
With energy galore.

We all go to midnight mass,
Our singing is just fine,
Grandma fancies the vicar,
And Grandad loves the wine.

Gerald Hampshire

THE HOLLY

Dark, shiny leaves, red berries galore
The garden adorned with holly once more
It does bear the crown on nature's fine head
Bringing the past alive from the dead.

In our busy Post Office, Mum and Dad toil,
Serving customers, young, old and loyal
Thud goes the date stamp as parcels and letters come and go
There's magic afoot, this I know.

Carollers arrive, their sweet voices sing
The church clock chimes and the bells ring
Out in the frosty night air
And by the fireside, Grandad sits in his chair.

A distant alarm wakes me with a jolt
My reminiscences brought to a halt.
I still have Cinderella lights, nearly sixty years old
With lots of stories as memories unfold.

Our little grandaughter will keenly listen
As the fairy lights twinkle and the frost will glisten.
The holly brings back those times of gladness
With just a touch of wistful sadness.

June Coral Dye

MYSTERY

In the beginning - a voice in the darkness.
'Let there be light'
and there was light;
and He declared it good.

And for a while it was good,
but then silently, stealthily,
the darkness crept back -
enveloping the Earth

Surely the voice would come again,
searing through the darkness -
commanding armies of angels
to reclaim His creation.

But what is this?
'Unto us a child is born'
a child? A baby?
this is His solution?

In the stillness of the night
the mystery is revealed.
We hold our breath . . .
in wonder.

Ruth Walker

SPARE A DIME

Christmas time's a special time
And one that we should share
When you hear the words 'spare a dime'
Just show them that you care.

The fairy sits upon the tree
She has her magic wand,
A symbolic angel is what I see
It fills my heart with song.

And Jesus born to me and you
To fill our children with laughter
A special gift from God it's true,
With love forever after.

Some are not so lucky
Not like you or I.
Take care that you should think of others
And make them smile not cry.

For Christmas time is special
A time when we should care
There's an abundance of love within our hearts,
It's time for us to share.

April Dickinson-Owen

FOOD FOR THOUGHT

Holly and mistletoe, tinsel and fun,
Christmas trees, baubles and more,
Mother has baked the pies and cakes,
Is there enough or should she bake more?

It's Christmas again,
The time of year when we buy presents galore.
A jumper for Dad,
Is it his size?
Will this perfume be right for Aunt Maude?

John wants a bike, Mary a doll,
Do its eyes open and close?
Is the fifteen pound turkey cooked tender or dry?
Buy good tights for Granny; fine hose.

The shops are all bursting with all we require
To make Yuletide go with a swing,
Carols are sung in melodious tone,
The bank balance looks a bit thin.

We will cope with card writing, overnight guests,
Almost all that the season entails,
But if two thousand years ago Jesus hadn't been born,
We wouldn't have Christmas today.

__Dorothy M Mitchell__

HEY, SANTA

Now listen here Santa I've something to say
I've heard that you're coming to ours Christmas Day
I'll make you some nibbles, my mum can help me
You'll find them beneath our Christmas tree
Tell 'Rudolph the reindeer' he won't be forgotten
We'll leave him a carrot and check it's not rotten
Make sure that you wipe your feet on the mat
And please don't step on Boris, our cat!
Now . . . I don't want much for Christmas this year
Cos I realise everything's getting too dear
I've asked for a skateboard, a watch and a bike
A brand new computer is what I would like
New jeans and a jumper, some socks and some shoes
A hat and some gloves is what I did choose
They must all have labels to give me 'street cred'
To make me look cool from my feet to my head
I'd like a new football to kick round the park
A torch that will help me see in the dark
Some sweets and some pens and some books I can read
These are all the things I really do need!
Mum says I've been good, but I can't have the lot,
But I know I'll be happy with whatever I got
Cos the thing I want most is what money can't buy
It's that Bubbles my goldfish (and friend) hadn't died!

Wendy Orlando & Emma Orlando (10)

It's That Time Of Year

The countdown has started,
The big rush is on.
People searching for gifts
Before the good ones are gone.

Lists growing larger,
Bank accounts shrinking.
Stores getting busier,
Do you get what I'm thinking?

It's the last weekend before Christmas,
Can you imagine the crowd?
Pushing and shoving,
And incredibly loud.

As much as I love Christmas,
I can't wait till it's over.
There's just too much hassle,
For all this bother.

In just 12 months time,
We'll do this all again.
But I'll be glad for the break,
Merry Christmas my friends!

Georgie Roomes

A Message Of Peace

Bright stars are twinkling there up in the dark sky,
As in a manger a newborn babe doth lie,
Mary and Joseph in that stable so bare,
Are watching over their child with tender care.

When a vision of angels light up the sky,
Fearful shepherds in haste to Bethlehem fly,
They have come from the fields where their sheep doth graze,
With much wonder and awe on this child they gaze.

He is the Lord of all the Earth and the sky,
This little babe that on the soft hay doth lie,
He has left the glory in the realm of Heaven,
A message of peace to lowly shepherds given.

Upon a wooden cross He came down to die,
For to save all of us 'tis the reason why,
Into this dark dreary world of sin and shame,
As a small helpless infant the Saviour came.

Bright stars are twinkling there up in the dark sky,
As in a manger a newborn babe doth lie,
In the stalls cows and oxen around Him stand,
As bright twinkling stars shine o'er all of the land.

Ruth Dewhirst

THROUGH A CHILD'S EYES

Christmas, full of surprises,
peace, goodwill to all.
Children excited, jumping with joy
that's what it's all about
seeing their faces light up on Christmas morn.
Oh! what a feeling to believe in that bearded man,
Santa Claus.

Christmas Eve night unable to sleep
heart's missing a beat.
Tiptoe, tiptoe,
ssh, whose are those feet?
Eyes peering over the sheets,
I hope you kids are asleep.
'Dad! When will Santa come?' they shout with delight.
'Will he eat our mince pie?'
'He might!'

When all is silent, peaceful and still
spare a thought for those less fortunate
who won't get a present or food to eat
nor family to visit, open presents around the tree.
Be thankful for good health, raise a glass,
make a wish, I know mine, what's yours?

Tracey Clayton

SONG FOR A TIME
(A song for a time when the sweet bells chime, calling rich and poor to pray, traditional carol)

A song for a time when the tills all chimed
For the rich and the poor to pay.
For Santa down the chimney climbed
Bringing gifts on Christmas Day.

Then through the door, in a month or more,
Will flood the letters you dread.
Mr Barclay wants you at half past four
For you're deep, deep, deep in the red.

Mr Lloyd is appalled that you never called
To repay the five grand he lent you gladly.
Now from his marbled hall you'll blackballed
For you've let him down so badly.

As for HSBC they are unable to see
How you've created a situation so drastic.
You're in such a mess they cannot say 'yes'
And have cut off all your plastic.

In the good old days when the bells rang out
We spent what we had, or we did without.
We gave only gifts that we could afford
And for what we received we thanked the Lord.

John Eccles

RED BREAST

Little robin at my window
Have you nowhere to hide?

It's snowing very heavy
Would you like to come inside?

You can sit inside my window
Or have warmth beside the fire

I could feed you with some bacon rind
You can eat to your desire

Your red breast is so beautiful
It burns against the snow

Could it be the story's true
From wenst came that fiery glow?

They say you sat beneath the Cross
The day that man was blessed

A drop of blood from crown of thorns
It fell against your breast

The story had a happy end
As Christ's spirit rose to Heaven

He left us with His memory
To you a red breast was given

Nicky Anderson

THE REASON FOR THE SEASON

It's Christmas time, it's that time of year
For parties and families and seasonal cheer
But behind it all lies Christ's incarnation
For God became Man to procure our salvation
The word became flesh for sinful women and men
And came as a baby to old Bethlehem
Father Christmas, in truth, is only a fable
The Gospel is true - Jesus was born in that stable
The story is greater than mere tongue can tell
The wonder of wonders - Emmanuel
God loved the world so, that His own Son He gave
Christ Jesus came, for us sinners to save
Three and thirty years later, on an old rugged tree
Christ died for sinners, at dark Calvary
There on that Cross, He did shed His own blood
To reconcile sinners like us, back to God
In Him alone, we are sure we're forgiven
By Him alone, have we right to God's Heaven
Be most careful then of mere frivolous mirth
And ponder the reason why Christ came to Earth
Unless that old Cross overshadows the manger
To God's own grace, you will just be a stranger
Christmas Day's coming - but soon it is past
Yet the blessing of Christ for eternity lasts
Apart from God's mercy you surely are lost
Give thanks for that baby - give thanks for the Cross.

Timothy Cross

IT'S CHRISTMAS SOON

I wonder . . . does Mummy know it's Christmas soon?
At play school I'm learning a Christmas tune
In the kitchen busy rolling mince pies
Mummy is sighing the loudest of sighs

I don't understand why - she hasn't got much to do
Father Christmas does it all - I'm pretty sure that's true
I thought I saw him the other day you know
With a trolley filled with toys at the local Tesco

All those presents to deliver to girls and boys
It's clever how he knows who wants what toys
I'm sending him a letter this very night
As Mummy reads it she's turning quite white

I told her, 'Father Christmas will bring it for sure
What won't come down the chimney he'll leave by the door.'
Why is Daddy giving that funny look?
As Mummy hides behind her book

I've so much to do, writing my cards and learning my play
There aren't enough hours in the day
What Mummy does all day I really don't know
It's *me* who is always on the go

My name is Thomas and I'm just three
Wondering what Father Christmas will bring me.

Judie Archer

CHRISTMAS

So why do I keep falling for this madness every year?
It's ludicrous - insanity - the very fact I'm here
With all this Christmas wrapping which will blatantly be torn
From parcels that take days to pack and lovingly adorn.

And how can I repeat each year that cardinal mistake
Of bothering to marzipan and ice a rich fruit cake
Which no one even contemplates - besides the sorry fact,
My all important effort, six months later, sits intact!

And when I think of how I rush to organise by nine
That wretched Christmas turkey to be cooked and served on time
So those who like to hear the Queen and those who want to walk
Can please themselves - do what they like, without a second thought

To what goes on behind the scenes, as panic takes a hold
'Did someone put the pudding in?'
'The veg is almost cold!'
'How could the cranberry sauce be lost?'
'Why won't these cracker's bang?'
Then morbidly, I wonder why we bother asking Gran!

But I resolve to change it all when New Year rings its chimes
This is, I vow, the final time I'll vacuum the pines
That are clogging up the Hoover pipe and sticking to my soles
To be away for Christmas, heads my list for 'next year's goals'!

Jo Lewis

WELL, IT'S CHRISTMAS . . . ISN'T IT?

Shopping in the supermarket,
Stuffing, sausages, the joint,
Spending money, so much money,
What's it for? What is the point?
Crackers with a toy inside them,
Christmas napkins, cloth to match,
Centre-piece with candle burning,
Children all with colds to catch,
Presents packed in pretty paper,
Parcels placed beneath the tree,
Purchases of passing beauty
For people who no longer see.
Our eyes are blind to sights from Heaven.
Our ears don't hear words from above.
Our hearts are beating only
At the pulse rate of a selfish love.
How far we've come from that first Christmas.
How our hearts have lost the joy!
Hope has vanished - hopeless future
Here without that baby boy.
Comfy, cosy, Christ-less Christmas,
Crates of beer and cans of Coke,
Cards on sideboards, cardboard greetings,
Annual ritual. Annual joke?

Sally Drury

CLOUDED BY SADNESS

Christmas comes but once a year
The world celebrates with festive cheer
The exchanging of presents and Christmas delight
Religious festivities that feel so right

A celebration for all to enjoy
Children playing with many a toy
Families gathering, folk in search of sun
Unaware disaster would strike, no longer deserving of such fun.

A great sadness has engulfed the whole world
The tsunami waves have greatly swirled
Death and destruction, sadness and tears
Everyone is affected, a nation with fears
A catastrophic event, suffered by all
The world is united, and will stand tall

The rescue operation is underway
Heads of state having their say
Thoughts and prayers are with the bereaved
So too with rescue teams, for what they have achieved

Aid will be provided, to restore what has been lost
That will amount to a significant cost
Money means nothing, as the nation will not forget
The Christmas clouded with sadness, dismay and regret

Jo Lees

CHRISTMAS

Glittering streets, sparkling shop windows, decorated Christmas trees
Father Christmas strolling the arcades
Folks thronging in the stores
Marvelling at the most latest technology
From mobile phones, TV sets, computers, cameras and camescopes
To the newly fashionable attires
While the little child in the manger
Lies waiting for thousands who no more turn out.

The commemoration of the birth of Jesus
Christians by the thousands care less
In today's troubled world
Merry-making is becoming more common than piety
In gluttonous eating and drinking
Lavishing money in gifts by tradition
So inconsistent are these to the life of Jesus
Like so many things associated with Christmas
Nativity scenes have become big business
Rows of shops sell figures for nativity scenes
Some of the more popular ones represent modern-day celebrities
Not characters from Gospel accounts
Christmas has become a universal holiday
An enchanting time of festive fun
We all glorify
And around which we all revolve
Sadly Christmas . . . has lost Christ!

Dan Chellumben

MESSAGE OF JOY

Christmas. Snow . . .
deep and crisp and even;
just like a childhood dream.

Candles glow,
softening the dark around us.
Christmas tree dressed in green.

Children know
the story of the manger.
A baby born. A star. Three kings.

Love flows
from house to house, to house.
Message of joy, carried on angel's wings.

Christmas glow
lighting people's faces . . .
as, for the special birthday, we all wait.

Rich or poor,
the magic draws us close,
'til bells and carols the silence break.

'Tis Christmas
snow,
deep and crisp and even . . .
just like a childhood dream.

Patricia Spear

THE CHRIST OF CHRISTMAS

Dear infant Lord! Come, sleep awhile
And rest before the day,
Upon Your manger bed of straw,
While wondering shepherds pray,
And angel hosts exalt their Lord,
Triumphal in the hay.

Dear Virgin Mother of our Lord
Who looks with marvelling gaze,
Upon Your holy Child of grace,
With heart of love and praise,
What bliss ineffable is Yours
For everlasting days!

Dear foster Father of our Christ,
What holy joy is yours,
To be the guardian of the Lord
Whom every heart adores,
And peace sublime was on your time,
Which God our King outpours.

Dear saints and sages from afar,
In prayer before the Child,
Praise Him, the Wisest of the Wise,
And only undefiled,
The power and wisdom of our God,
With mercy underpiled.

Derek Sones

JOYEUX NOEL

Once again the time is here,
time for happiness, time for cheer!
Christmas trees and Christmas cards,
from front room walls to doctor's wards!
It's a time for love and time for giving,
time for family and comfort living.
Although there is some spiritual aspect,
this is a time for one's reflection.
Receiving gifts that you wouldn't expect,
symbols of love and affection.
Whatever you do or wherever you are,
someone cares for you from the bottom of their hearts!
Turkey on the table, gravy and wine,
for everybody's plate, but I want it for mine!
The chaos of Christmas has yet to end,
the Christmas card you forgot to send,
is lying on the shelf ready to be posted,
while you lay back by fire, feet getting roasted!
Six in the evening and the light starts to fade,
the dinner's been eaten and the table's all made.
Feet up on the sofa and the crackers been pulled,
you get out your cups for the wine that is mulled!
Christmas is over, for another year waiting,
the rest of the year is another one hating.
But New Year's Eve is only one week,
a new resolution you will now have to seek!

Joseph Larkin

CHRISTMAS SHOPPING

It's the season for children of all ages
Shops filled with brand new toys
Looking in the windows with gleeful faces
Such delights all stacked for girls and boys.

Anticipation of what's about to happen
Santa will soon be arriving in the shop
Letters to write promising to be very good
Hoping that at their house he'll stop.

In the brightly coloured windows stacked
Dolls, teddies, cars, tractors and every game
Little faces against the glass, noses pressed
Hoping on one will be their own name.

Santa sits in his snow-covered grotto
Children queue to see him, looking in awe
Lists are endless of toys they are wanting
Such a mammoth task in store for them all.

Excited children wanting this and that
Running along to every shop
Mums and Dads getting more exhausted
Shopping on until they drop.

Christmas morning to see their faces
Great excitement as they gather around the tree
Presents of every shape and size
Shouting, 'Please, is there one for me?'

Gill D'Arcy

THE SNOWFLAKE CATCHER

When I was putting my house to bed
For no more than an Earthly second was I led
Into a reflection, into a dream,
Into a world I'd never seen,
I caught snowflakes and held them in my hand,
They trickled through my fingers and turned to sand.
Golden rains gathered at my feet. Swirling magic for me to greet.
On their regal trains I trod,
As we gazed skyward towards the little god.
In my caravan of dreams, on this trip to other lands
I held hands with Gabriel, an angel not a man.
He took the stars; light in his cloak,
Casting the mantle across the globe upon the simple folk.
Who he conspired with I do not know, the light touched only goodness,
Sadly the world was not all aglow.
It danced on presents that showed thought
And Christmas trees in New York,
It danced on old ladies' memories and a man taking his dog for a walk.
We travelled to Norway and even Budapest,
Our second was precious and left no time for rest.
When he had gathered all the feelings and the thoughts,
Gabriel scattered them in Bethlehem and left them for the angels to sort.
The star grew bright glowing from goodness collected this night.
Every eve since I've put my house to bed,
Hoping for Gabriel's touch, to no avail, in my hand glistens
A snowflake instead.

Gail Anselmi

AT CHRISTMAS

Church bells
sound the night air
high up in the belfry
calling for prayer.

Christmas Eve
when Jesus was born
rejoice and singing
oh happy morn

Alight are the eyes
of children so young
on Christmas Day
that's when it begun

The gifts we give
and also receive
make Christmas special
festivities cheer

A long time ago
when Jesus was young
Bethlehem blessed us
and gave us a Son

We stand by tradition
and celebrate
the Christmas festival
in His name sake.

Margery Rayson

CHRISTMAS IS BLISS

Christmas is this - bliss!
The letting go of all that keeps us low.
Forgiving our own hearts for lack of love.
Thanking God for pathways trod by many others before us,
Leaving channels clear for me and you to ask Jesus to help us
To be who we are and the best of that.
To understand what love is,
To help us heal our wounds concealed and open the doors
For growth and understanding of our small worlds.

Christmas is this - bliss!
To say it's OK for me not to know and let you be who you are
And care for you regardless of your sin, 'tis not mine
To pray each day for those whose path has led them into lessons hard
Sometimes too much to bear and not care about what you have,
But love you all the same and give all of me to you
And gather strength from God to do so as you hate me in your pain.

Christmas is this - bliss!
To stop and take time out to see the song of life eternally
And thank God for the sky, the trees, the birds, the wind,
Good food and ease that sits within my life, my health and
All the freedoms that I have and ask that those who don't enjoy,
Are blessed with such whatever is their name for God,
As mine is that inside my heart. To sit on Christmas morn in light
And say in joyous prayer: Happy Birthday Jesus,
Thanks be to God you're there.

Susan E Powell

CHRISTMAS FAIRY

I am the Christmas fairy
on the Christmas tree,
where human hands have placed me
so they can admire me.

I look down on the baubles,
the tinsel and the beads,
the chocolate, the fairy lights
that flash from 'lectric leads.

Though none can hold a candle
to me, the Christmas queen
and though of royal blood I am
those humans treat me mean.

The twelfth night of Christmas
I'm thrown into a box,
no one cares how bad I feel
or how this treatment shocks.

I'm forced to lie down with 'plebs'
and suffer indignation,
I'm pushed into a draughty loft
like some common decoration.

Eleven months of the year
I'm totally neglected,
but when December comes around
I'm suddenly respected!

Pandy Pond

WHITE CHRISTMAS

'Twas during the Christmas morning 2004,
That snowflakes came fluttering at our door.
Slowly at first, then with increasing speed,
The surrounding landscape did recede
Under a chilly blanket of sparkling white,
Much to a lot of people's delight.
At lower altitudes it didn't stay long,
Just time to cause a stir, then it was gone,
But 'twas a different story upon the moorland high,
Where the craggy granite tors reach up towards the sky,
There among the rocks where ponies, sheep and cattle graze,
The wintry covering lasted for a number of days.
Thousands of eager travellers journeyed to the moors,
Each fed up with being cooped up indoors.
Some arrived with sledges, others with tin trays,
One or two flew their kites; there was fun to be had in many ways.
Many built snowmen; others had a snowball fight,
Yet more carried cameras to record the breathtaking sight.
Forget all the presents, the toys and the rest,
This was something you couldn't buy; it was nature at its best.
As the sun slowly sank, glowing fiery red,
Revellers returned to their cars to journey home in time for bed
And through the blue and pink misty eastern sky,
A dazzling moon rose to light the wonderland from on high.
The snow had brought such pleasure, who could ask for more?
Many will remember the white Christmas of 2004.

Margaret Blight

CHRISTMAS DAY

Christmas Day has dawned at last
Forget the panic - it's all in the past
The sense of excitement is now all around
Half awake you hear laughter as presents are found

The kitchen becomes the centre of activity
As the turkey is cooked with a well-stuffed cavity
The steamer is ready for the large Christmas pud
You'd preserve all those smells, if only you could!

And all through the morning the family call by
With presents for Johnny, Aunt Kathy and Vi
They stop for a sherry, mince pie and a chat
And with kisses and hugs move on to Aunt Pat

Then somebody shouts, 'It's starting to snow'
And you all watch with wonder through the nearest window
The flakes fall down quietly and start getting bigger
Sticking to walls and laying much thicker

A robin appears on the gatepost nearby
His red breast ablaze as he swoops from the sky
He's eager to take all the crumbs that's been strewn
Snow fell unannounced on this afternoon

As this perfect day ends, and the darkness comes down
Mum looks out from the door in her new dressing gown
She sees Christmas lights like stars in the night
Reflecting their colour on a carpet of white

Christine Shelley

I'D LOVE TO BE AN ANGEL

I'd love to be an angel in our school play,
Or to be Mary and have loads of lines to say,
But Charlotte got Mary and the angels are all cast,
When Teacher read out who had parts my name was last,
I'm to play 'the donkey' typical though,
I never get a decent part in our school show.

I was 'chorus member' last year I didn't do a lot,
But Teacher says that this year I should be glad of what I've got,
But I'd love to be an angel all dressed in white,
Teacher says I can understudy in case someone's ill that night,
So I'm praying every day that Lucy's sick in bed,
Someone else can play the donkey I'll be an angel instead.

Me Mam says, 'Don't get excited,' that, 'we'll have to wait and see,'
But I've already made a halo from the tinsel off the tree,
I'd love to be an actress, an angel's a good start,
I've taken home the script and learnt the words off by heart,
And I don't get discouraged when in choir they say I'm flat,
Cos the girl who plays Gabriel has a voice like a cat.

We were given our costumes yesterday, everyone else looked grand,
We tried them on in the sports hall and rehearsed with the band,
I wear an old rug and a shoebox on my head,
And all I do is clip-clop round the stage and lie down
                                              in what looks like a shed,
It's supposed to be a stable but the caretaker made it too small,
I hope I'm an angel next year, the costume won't fit if I grow too tall.

Alison Gorton

OH WHERE DID CHRISTMAS GO?

Midnight mass on Christmas Eve
freezing fingers tucked up your sleeve
snow is falling all around
excited kids' eyes big and round.
Oh where did Christmas go?

Church bells ring on Christmas morning
jump out of bed without even yawning.
Did he come? Has he been?
Look he left me a tangerine.
Oh where did Christmas go?

Granny comes round with a box of games
she's so funny she forgets our names.
A great big dinner, can I have a leg?
Too many grown ups so you have to beg.
Oh where did Christmas go?

Dinner's finished off with trifle and jelly
all is quiet for the Queen on the telly
argue with sisters, they're cheating at draughts
moan to Dad but he just laughs.
Oh where did Christmas go?

Now I'm grown up with children to feed
and all I get is Dad I need
a stereo, a telly, a DVD screen.
Whatever happened to the tangerine?
Oh where did Christmas go?

John Simpson

SANTA MAGIC

Dear Santa, I want to tell you,
What you need to know,
I've written out my wish list,
Of toys I've seen on show.

There's the latest Harry Potter,
There's the newest mobile phone,
It has all the gadgets,
Wouldn't that be cool, just magic.

Then there's the action videos
And DVDs as well,
I've listed all the titles,
But don't want the one with Schmeichel.

I also want a brand new bike,
With all the gears and all the lights,
Now if there's still room in your sack,
For a flat screen computer with fast track.

My mum says I want too much,
But deciding on less is pretty tough,
For a boy has to keep abreast,
So I really couldn't do with less.

Dear Santa, my dad has just read this letter, he said,
'Can you think of more or do any better?
If Santa brings you all this stuff,
There'll be no presents for the rest of us.'

Elizabeth Hiddleston

A Modern Christmas Carol

No Christmas at our house this year
Cos Santa's in the jug.
He got careless with his shopping
And they videoed his mug.
He explained it was just an impulse
And he was in a state of shock
He really had no idea of the time.
Early morning, really? Four o'clock!
He was just borrowing the tele'
To see if it would fit;
If it was too big
He'd be returning it;
But if it was the right size
He'd be calling back to pay.
He was coming up to town
The very, very next day.
The goodies in his pocket?
Must have fallen off the shelf.
What did he need with gin and whisky?
He was a teetotaller himself;
But the constable that nicked him
Must have been a cynical man;
Though I rather think what clinched it
Was Dad loading a five ton van.
No Christmas at our house this year
Cos Santa's in the jug.
At least he'll be happy there
They provide a better class A drug.

Terry Ireland

GIVING TO RECEIVE

Joy in receiving,
Diminishes with knowing,
Many motives not seen as a child:
Obligation, profit, controlling minds, unwanted holidays,
Allow memory time,
So comparisons are drawn,
Then erased by tears.

Because the meal is not so filling
And less excitement and effort made,
And gifts bring little joy.
Thought, yes, how nice! But no longer for play,
The gift says, 'More important things
To consider for you today.'

Yet, once again, togetherness!
We, here, bless!
Not Christian son nor pagan solstice,
But my kin and your kin sharing all this,
Getting cold, getting warm, festive flavours, mulled wine,
Ignoring debt, consumerism, lack of faith, just a while.
So we enjoy and smile!

Seeing more joy in receiving,
(Not to tell is not deceiving)
More joy we bring by giving,
Brings happiness.
We are content so, not to change,
This festival deranged.

Hugh Ortega Breton

SANTA'S VISIT

Santa half fell down the chimney
(The last one left in the street).
He'd had a few mince pies and whiskeys
And wasn't too steady on his feet.
He picked up the note they had left him
But couldn't make out what it said.
The letters and words were a jumble
Cos the whiskey had gone to his head.
He plopped himself down on the sofa
He was sorely in need of a rest
He searched in his bag for some presents
And sighed, 'I'm just doing my best!'
He was still there early next morning
When the children jumped out of their bed -
The sound of their feet on the stairway
Gave him such a pain in his head.
Santa just made it back to the chimney
As the children entered the room,
But instead of delight at their presents
The youngsters were covered in gloom.
They hadn't requested bath smellies,
Nor hankies, nor socks labelled *'Dad'*
Santa heard them complain at their presents
And say that they felt they'd been had.
So in future when you leave a message
Telling Santa to leave what he *oughta!*
Remember - don't pour him a whiskey
Just leave him a tumbler of water.

H Lamb

CHRISTMAS 2005

We e-mailed to Santa, but got no reply
His laptop was buried
Under presents, I wonder why?
'Please send me a computer,' I begged
'A mouse and a printer.'
I want to keep busy
Cos now it is winter.
Santa came with a cheque for me
And a note, *I'm sorry your present*
Has been held up in the post.
The sales were all on and the very next day
I bought my computer and took it away.
I'm busy in winter, my mouse is worn out
There's a competition to enter, I know what it's all about
It's to take people's minds off the flood waves and turmoil
Those poor helpless children and the adults too
The tsunami came to take them
Away from our world.
And so Father Christmas, I hasten to say
Many thanks for the present and
If I win this competition, I'll help them without delay.
Their aid is important and my help only small
At present that is - until I win it all.
I don't need the money. I've got a computer
For those long, weary nights at Christmas
With my header and footer.
So let us be thankful for our electricity bill
We have light, power and poems to feed the soul within.

Joan Peacock

CHRISTMAS SLEIGHING

Careless whispers at Christmas time
Then cursing the words to Auld Lang Syne
People push the Christmas cheer
But it's simply not my time of year
Okay, I know I'm sounding off
It's easy for you to sit and scoff
Then stand and shout
And pull your cracker
The constant sound
Of relative chatter
But you've got to have faith
Understand my reason
Summertime leads to ultimate
Freedom

So keep your snow
Your Santa's hat
The usual gifts of Christmas tat
Forget the choir
Your songs of glee
Unwrappings strewn around the tree
Do you get my meaning
My point, you see?
The long cold nights
Are not for me
My time of year
My place to be
Club Tropicana
Where drinks are free.

Mark Guy

POEM FOR CHRISTMAS

When does the tree go up Mum? Tell me again,
When does Father Christmas come?
Oh I can't wait till then!
The excitement on their faces,
Anticipation in the air,
Of course they have long forgotten,
The real story they should share.

So I spend my time trying to explain, again and again,
Exactly what Christmas is all about?
But I might as well shout
With all the hype that's about!
From September to December,
It's shops full of Christmas cheer.

All they are after is your money,
Money you don't have to spare,
So I'll carry on in my own sweet way, this year,
As usual it'll be the same,
Christmas with the children,
Always the same poor old way.

Small turkey on the table,
Cheap crackers for the pulling there,
Candles that have seen better days,
It is wonderful, because,
But plenty of love all around us,
Love is in the air!

Janet Hopkins

CAN'T WAIT FOR CHRISTMAS

I will have a magical Christmas
Like everyone I have ever known.
They say it's a time for children,
Well I'm a child, just overgrown.
On the hearth I leave mince pies and sherry
Just as my parents showed me.
My husband thinks I am stupid,
(He gets up to devour them, about 3)
I still have my advent calendar
A chocolate behind each window.
I look forward to Christmassy milk tops
And hope for a frost if not snow.
I still take the kids carol singing
Traditions I just can't let go
Like the money in Christmas pudding
And Morecambe and Wise Christmas show.
I love those chocolate novelties
That hang on the tree with gold thread,
Nuts and mandarin oranges
And candy canes striped in red.
My kids now too old for Santa
Try hard not to spoil it for me.
They hang up their stocking by fireside
Their amusement is obvious to see.
Uncomplaining, they go to bed early
So I can distribute presents unseen,
I have to be up nice and early
Frantically screaming
He's been!

Jennifer Oxley

ANGELS CAROLLING HYMNS

If Jesus was born today, it would be a different sight
Surrounded by midwife and nurses
In a hospital, noisy and bright:
Mary would sit up in bed, cup of tea and crib at her side,
The babe in blue cotton shawl
Her hope, her joy, her pride;
Gift bearers at visiting time, their cards and flowers would bring
Knitted toys, bibs, tiny socks
Silver trinkets, a horse that rocks,
But no choir of angels to sing:

If Jesus were born tomorrow, it would be a different affair
Surrounded by android machines
With stainless steel everywhere:
Mary would be a bystander, an incubator taking her place
She'd gaze at Him through a window
And long to touch His face;
Gift bearers won't need to arrive, virtual cards and flowers they'll send
Digital imaged balloon
Free tickets for trips to the moon
But no shepherds down hills will descend:

Jesus was born yesterday, a poor but glorious occasion
Surrounded by animals only
In a stable, close ruination:
Joseph was at Mary's side, a manger sufficed for a bed
A star shone out up on high
To show where the babe lay His head:
Gift bearers came in great haste, shepherds heralding kings
Lambs brought down from the hills, gold from great boxes spills
Incense and myrrh the air filled
Angels carolling hymns:

Elizabeth Bowes

CHRISTMAS

I love Christmas!
I've loved Christmas for most of my long life.
Not so much for the festivities and the fun,
Though that is all part of it,
Or for the expectancy of Advent-time,
Or the fast-growing exuberance of the lights,
The over-eating, and the excessive drinking,
Certainly not for the buying of expensive presents,
Although giving and receiving is an integral part of it,
I love Christmas for the special joy abroad at the season,
Most of all for the fact that my daughter was born on Christmas Eve.
I loved the velvet darkness of the sky
As I cycled nightly to the maternity hospital,
The spangled counterpane of twinkling stars.
I sensed it was something like this
On that first ever eastern Christmas in Palestine
When Mary and Joseph journeyed hurriedly to Bethlehem,
It must've seemed as if creation was putting on
A picture show to welcome that special birth.
I, also, expected the crescent moon to leap with joy,
And the twinkling stars to dance in ecstasy.
The sound of angels would be very welcome,
Heavenly music with its wonderful burden of peace.
O happy, magic times of joy so unconfined!
A healthy baby, and burgeoning love abroad!
When Christmas entered my heart, and the world sang!
I love Christmas!

Jack Scrafton

REVELATION

Do we need to have a word
    to explain it?
Must we cringe from
    having to find it?
What drives the quest
    for things that don't exist?
Questions from confusion
    asked of an analyst
assumed to have
    the expertise of discovery
delving to find
    our shrouded mystery.

We are left groping
    to find a panacea
making all the haunted
    pasts disappear.
Searching for an ever
    shrinking talisman
by putting our trust
    in a phantom helmsman.
Turn of card, fall of coin
    giving a chance of choosing.
Bets placed against
    the shattered hopes of winning.

We tread our way through terrains
    flint edged and wild
privileged to witness
    the birth of a child.

Michael Fenton

CHRISTMAS ON THE BEACH

My daughter nagged 'til I was numb
'Oh come on Mum, it will be fun,'
But I didn't think it would be that neat
To spend Christmas melting in searing heat

We took the presents on the plane
But somehow it's just not the same
Their Christmas tree was nice enough
But I like snow and ice and stuff

When Christmas morning came at last
I woke to an air-conditioning blast
No central heating turned up high
I drew back curtains to blue sky

I'm used to cooking all day long
Not heating charcoal and brandishing tongs
No turkey, stuffing or Brussels sprouts
'Twas burgers, kebabs and raw bean sprouts

After lunch there was no time for sitting
Watching TV, reading or knitting
It was to the beach with towel and bathers
Straight into the ocean - nobody wavered

I laid out my towel and relaxed on the sand
No remote control growing hot in my hand
Perhaps I shouldn't have been quick to judge
This certainly beat my traditional drudge

So next year when I'm at home again
Staring at drizzle through windowpanes
I'll remember this Christmas and how I fussed
But tradition, like turkeys can always be stuffed!

Tamsin Quantrell

SOLITARY STAR

I scurried to the store
for the last gift
on my list.

The air grew cold
and frost landed on
my lip.

Finis.
At last . . . home.
I drew a bath
and lit a balsam candle.

I gazed up
at the darkness
of the night sky
and there - a solitary star
stared back at me.

A quiet star
in a silent sky,
was this the meaning
of Christmas?
A star that guided
royalty to a manger
one night?

The silent peace
of a dark sky
lit by an infinite candle - a solitary star
gazed back at me.

Elizabeth C Millar

STARLIGHT EXPRESS

The joy of Christmas, I believe,
Lies, not in the wining and the dining,
The feasting and the making merry,
No killjoy am I,
For these gladsome things are very necessary.

An expression of the truest joy,
Discovering that no longer need we victims be
Of the downward pull of our carnal nature,
A startling revelation,
That our loving Heavenly Father's gift to us
Was invented as a plan for our salvation!

When we were powerless to help ourselves,
As helpless and dependent as that baby in the manger,
God had sent His 'only begotten son' in human form,
An incredible pathway and escape route to the stars
Had in fact been forged,
And it was ours!

We only needed to lift our heads high,
Open our hearts and our hands to Him,
Receive that Christ child into our lives
Let Him take control
And the power and the glory
Would tell their own story.

The joy of Christmas, I believe
Lies, not in the dining and the making merry,
The carolling, the home, the hearth, candles at midnight,
Glasses of sherry,
It can be found in the quiet secret places of a reflective heart,
Which once was sad, now made glad!

Beryl Moorehead

JINGLE ALL THE WAY

There is something special,
that comes on Christmas Day.
It's more than words and presents,
that brings happiness our way.

Watch the weans on Christmas morn,
as the Christmas tree they'll pause,
and search to find their presents,
left by Santa Claus.

There's the stockings on the mantelpiece
full of fruit and things that's sweet.
Except the one that's Daddy's,
it's full of holes to air his feet.

You scratch your head in wonder.
What's in their heads this day?
Once they've looked inside their parcels,
it's with the boxes, that they play.

Once you've had your dinner,
you must find a comfy seat,
as your tummy has expanded,
and you can nae see your feet.

Of course there are other people
who sell all these festive things,
though they don't believe in Christmas,
love the wealth it always brings.

With their pockets full of money.
Think Santa Claus is swell.
As they look at their empty shelves
where there's nothing left to sell.

Ian W Wilkinson

AT LAST I KNEW

When I was young Christmas was about a glow.
I didn't know what it was; I was much too young to know.
All I know is that my smile was a mile wide.
The happiness felt as if it would burst from inside.

As I grew older, I began to wonder what it was all about.
I watched as Christmas was degraded, enough to make you shout.
People became so greedy they simply just lost the sight.
All they want now are presents and Christmas to be white.

Christmas is a loving time, to share with family and friends.
Jesus gave his life for us, upon us He now depends.
As I sat in church with my father listening to the mass,
I had this funny feeling of how Christmas came to pass.

The greatest gift any person can give,
Is the life in which they live.
That is what Jesus gave to us, the gift of His life and love,
That is what we must remember when we look to the sky above.

If Jesus can give all of Himself surely we can give just a bit.
So next time you're upon a bus let the old lady sit.
Help your children to give and not just to receive.
Guide them to be honest and not to deceive.

For the future of Christmas lies in their tiny hands.
As they grow older they will face many unfair demands.
They will have to get the balance right and this is hard to do.
But this is what makes us human the likes of me and you.

So remind yourself of what Christmas time is really for.
It's not just the day itself it's so much bloody more.
It's about how you live your life and the path that you choose.
So live your life for all it's worth or only you will lose.

Tom Roach

CHRISTMAS ANGEL

What does an angel look like?
Forget the wings, the halo, the golden trumpet,
the white flannelette nightgown.
Forget the seraphim and cherubim,
the thrones, dominations, virtues,
powers and principalities.
Angels resemble you and me,
except that they are a tad more angelic.

Some, according to Genesis, look like wrestlers.
Some, according to Tobit, like guides,
couriers, travel representatives.
Some, especially when in the vicinity
of inns, stables and empty tombs,
resemble BBC announcers,
with trim moustaches, butterfly bow ties
and pukkah, cut-glass, received pronunciation.

Some, according to Isaiah, remove coals
from the fire and place them against your lips
à la the bread and wine of communion.
Seven of them - Raphael, Michael, Gabriel
and the rest - have names and proper job descriptions.
They travel from the City of God to Nazareth
constantly repeating the Sanctus:
Holy, Holy, Holy is the Lord of Hosts.

Angels are messengers of the mystery of grace.
They are both wonderful and ordinary,
rather like you and me. Small deeds of kindness,
in the street or in the shops, are trumpet blasts
pointing to God. This red-nosed lady from the Sally Ann
might well be one, rattling her tambourine.

Norman Bissett

THE DOUBLE TASTES OF CHRISTMAS TIME

Christmas! It's Christmas time;
world's principal festive occasion,
happiest and busiest time of the year,
when a tree does not make a forest,
people enjoy the fruits of hard work
with friends, loved ones, family members,
holidaying and touring around the world,
even a time to explore the gifts of nature.

Oh! Sweet, sweet bitter moment: the double
tastes of Christmas time, when people
from all nooks and crannies make
save journeys, like the biblical save
journeys of the magi to Jerusalem
when Christ was born, today amidst tragic
tragic road accidents, as tragic as the
biblical killing of all male babies by King Herod.

The double tastes of Christmas time;
some eating and drinking, like in the
days of biblical Noah before the deluge,
others suffering, starving and weeping,
under economic hardships and natural disasters,
like the tsunami disaster in Asia,
oh, where tens of thousands of people died
coincidentally, this Christmas time.

The double tastes of Christmas time;
positive and negative, laughing and crying,
some buying Christmas goodies, some buying nothing,
some embracing morality, some kissing immorality,
some helping the poor, others abhorring the poor,
some eating and drinking moderately, others excessively.

Justice N Okafor

THE CHRISTMAS MASQUERADE

Shall I don my cloak of a hypocrite, yet again?
Pretending, pleasing those nearest and dearest to me.
Laugh like that Cavalier with the cruel, farcical smile?
Or should I try just that bit harder, to break free?

Then I think of the children, the new toys and the grottoes,
tearing parcels 'neath the spruce on Christmas morning.
Gorging tangerines and chocolates, searching for some new batteries,
as Santa and their mum's flaked out and yawning.

Spare some thoughts for the suicidal, depressed and the
                                                extremely lonely,
suffering dread throughout this period, and so alone.
During this, our season of peace, goodwill to all mankind,
compassionate Samaritans; waiting, manning phones.

But it's such a magical time of turkey and tinsel,
Christmas markets, mince pies and mulled wine.
Now even Frosty the snowman dances and sings,
and the lantern-carrying carol singers all rhyme in time.

Decorations and mistletoe draped elegantly from the ceilings,
Christmas stockings on the mantel with special cards.
Fireplaces prepared, milk and mince pies for Santa.
Rudolph's driving the packed sleigh and reindeer hard.

There'll still be large crowds of people, abundance of excess stock,
at the Boxing Day sales in Woolworth's stores.
If the capitalist weren't so greedy with their Chinese-made goods,
surely some unfortunates could afford to buy more?

The whole point of my poem? It's Christmas!
The birthday of the miraculous Nazarene,
Jesus Christ, Our Lord, God and Saviour,
and The Holy Ghost that's all around us, that can't be seen.

Tommy McBride

'FOR UNTO US A CHILD IS BORN'

Some psychologists insist that children must be allowed
to play with other children, it's in their nature, endowed
with a sense of meeting their age group, others of their years,
what it is, the experts know, young children present less fears.

To see a face still innocent, a ready smile, a light,
they glow with expectation, a friend they'll find, someone nice.
So readily drawn to features, no glumness or despair,
no worried frowns, complexions, with too many chores to care.

The attraction of young people, drawn together, should be
seen in the light of experience, letting them be free
instead of hindering friendships, supervision is wise
and parents who accept this draw their children to their sides.

The parent who is demanding; the world is over much,
does not make children welcome, however long their life, church
or home where they've grown, should reflect the joy of
                                                    their presence;
worlds or homes without children, sterile, unfriendly, a pretence.

The pretence to know what life is, parents or some other
cannot show their wisdom if a childless world they prefer.
When God blesses a couple, with one, their own healthy kind,
these the parents educate, are protectors for all time.

Why should others have the pleasure, scheduling all their days,
destroys the family bonding, drives their children away.
So fraught with all the demands, anxieties and exams,
unless their child is streamlined, parents feel they've failed their lambs.

If we could all be as children, though lived a hundred years,
our presence to any neighbour, possibly lessen fears?
This desert world without kindness, ourselves manna-like, feed
the whole wide world, starving, denied what they need 'cause of greed.

Gerasim

WAITING FOR SANTA

It is Christmas Eve and I just can't wait,
For Santa Claus to come down the chimney,
I am so excited, my letter has been sent,
Will I get what I really, really want?

Mum keeps telling me to go to sleep, 'cause
Santa only comes to little ones who are sound asleep,
It isn't easy to sleep, my thoughts and hopes
Are racing all over the place.

On the top of the tree the star is shining bright,
Outside the carollers are singing with great joy,
From the ethereal sky, there is a golden glow, a light,
Telling of the birth of a baby boy.

The name of this boy was Jesus,
Son of God, Jesus was later to give his life,
For those He loved,
Christmas is a time to remember His abiding love.

I like when Mum tells this story,
Never get tired of hearing it.
There's something so comforting about it,
Soon I drifted into a world of dreams.

The morning sun beaming through the window,
Wakened me to the delights left by Santa Claus,
My regret being that I had missed him again,
But the presents he left soon made me forget that.

After breakfast which I barely looked at,
Wanting to go out in the snow-covered landscape,
Where sledging down the hills was breathtaking,
Throwing snowballs at each other.
This is a happy day which I will long recall,
Hopes and dreams can come true with a little bother.

Mary Lawson

SANTA'S ADVENTUROUS JOURNEY

Far away from Lapland, Santa Claus is on his way
Speeding with his reindeers, upon the jolly sleigh
Ringing his bells so merrily with his jolly, 'Ho, ho, ho!'
The reindeers are already slipping, upon the glittering snow

Santa is proudly wearing his glasses, on the tip of his nose
Up to his tricks once again, I really do suppose
Knowing he will have something, up his jolly old sleeve
Upon this bitterly cold and frosty, jolly Christmas Eve

The reindeers then climb up a hill, and suddenly they jerk
Santa lets go of the reins, (well what a jolly berk!)
His glasses fall off his nose, as he slips down a slide
The reindeers look behind them, ears propped to one side

Santa climbs up the hill, back and forth, he's jolly sliding
The reindeers are there a-waiting, already they are shivering
Eventually, Santa found his glasses which took an hour or so
He's already covered with snow from head to his very toe

It's getting quite jolly late, as they arrive eventually
Santa gets stuck half-way down as he climbs down the chimney
It hadn't been swept at all, the soot came flying down
Santa came down black instead of white, feeling like a jolly clown

Children do not open your bedroom doors, even if you hear a noise
For jolly Santa will disappear and certainly be in disguise
The reindeers are waiting impatiently upon the roof so high
Just sleep soundly, for Christmas Day will soon be jolly nigh

Santa went to the reindeers and said, 'Am I really getting fat?'
Rudolph looked at him with surprise, so what do you think of that?
After a disastrous journey they went sliding back on land
Still singing with a jolly, 'Ho, ho, ho!' Feeling jolly well grand

They have to go back to Lapland where jolly wonders are there
Hoping Santa will be back next year with yet another adventure.

Jean P McGovern

HOME FOR CHRISTMAS

Oh do come to Christmas dinner at our house,
we have more than enough.
Yes of course you can bring your cardboard box,
bring along all of your stuff.
No stuff to bring! Oh maybe you can take some of ours.
We have so many presents for the kids, the unwrapping takes hours.
No money for presents. Sorry, did I hear you right, no money for food?
Look my dear chap, I don't mean to sound rude,
how do you get through Christmas without a drink and a meal?
Some people we know can eat so much, it can make you feel quite sick.

You'll be invited to your family's home.
What? They don't know where you are!
You live on the streets, is that right? What, even at night?
Abuse drove you away you say. Come on now,
shouting never hurt anyone.
I see, you won't tell me the whole story, much too violent and gory.

How can this be? No Christmas tree.
I find it hard to believe, with all the blessings I receive.
What gives me the right to have a life so enhanced?
Timing, my place of birth or purely chance.

For you, a season of loneliness and depression
while I try yet another fancy dress on.
Christmas night you might be blue from thoughts and the weather.
While we sing with our friends around our roaring log fire,
your Christmas time dire.
A room for family and unexpected guests we have to spare.
Blankets for you, we won't share
but give to you hopefully, to make your nights warmer.
Each year I spend a little less
because of people like you who are in a mess
you need help
and maybe because of the cards I've been dealt,
year by year, little by little, I can help.

Lesley Britton

CHRISTMAS ESSENTIALS

Cards and wrapping paper, calendars and decorations
For the Christmas tree
Dodging between crowds and traffic jams to the enticing
Displays in shops
Gifts for the young, having fun on Christmas morning,
Faces all aglow
On we go, hopping and dashing from crowded bus to
Visit Santa's grotto
With a jolly, 'Yo, ho, ho,' and a bewildering choice for
Girls and boys.
Toys, toys, toys and healthy options is the clarion cry of today
The family pet is encouraged to think thin,
Must not overdo the cat food or doggy tin.

Putting up the tree and tripping over the box of bargain baubles
That was too many anyway.
The spirit of the past is beaming out from some heart-warming
Old film on telly, festival kindliness and austerity and pastimes.
If you think all that has gone you are wrong.
The materialistic world is putting some positive thought into
The meaning of Christmas.

Dickens is remembered for a day, drawing crowds on market stalls
As people enact the past down a village street.
Frills and bonnets and frock coats, helpers on charity stalls.
A choir sings and a collection is made for the homeless.

Children in a country school hold a best-dressed Christmas tree lottery
And give what they make to buy a child they don't know a gift.
Lift the spirits of the freezing cold
With a clown making children laugh
An old fashioned scene brought to life by people coming out
And sparing a moment of their busy day to work a kind of magic
To strive and keep alive the essential warmth of Christmas.

Freda Grieve

CHRISTMAS SHOPPING BLUES

Christmas shopping gives me the blues
Have to join several long queues
All the checkouts are in demand
Hear the cries of a customer command
Hurry up or you'll be damned

I've been waiting for almost an hour
Someone in front needs a shower
Somebody pushes in ahead
Looks are given and they turn red

Then a customer's shopping falls on the floor
Tins, bottles and jars scatter, oh what a bore
Till has to close whilst they clear the mess
Voices raise and want redress

Looks like I'm here for quite a time
Haven't seen the outside since half-past nine
Now I have to join the end of another line
Assistant hands out free glasses of wine

Music fills the air
Terrible sounds make me despair
I feel like pulling out my hair
No one seems to bother or care

I'm in need of a tranquillising pill
Slowly the queue moves towards the till
Then a shoplifter refuses to foot the bill
I have just about had my fill

When at last I reach the checkout
I quickly pay by cash
Then I'm out the door in a flash
Free from the last minute dash

Peter G H Payne

CHRISTMAS

Christmas is a very busy time but also lots of fun
Mums and Dads all running around
Choosing presents for everyone
Lots of meals to arrange for all the festive days
At the end of it all it seems
The hard work really pays

Let's remember all our friends at this special time of year
Send best wishes to everyone
Wishing them health and good cheer
Enjoying the get-togethers with all the family ties
Fobbing off the little ones
Telling them lots of white lies

Preserving their belief in Father Christmas and his elves
And not to find the presents
Hidden amongst the shelves
Mind, we also want them to know the real Christmas story
All about the birth of Christ
Mary, Joseph and God's glory

Snow appearing will really make Christmas Day
Presents under the Christmas tree
Brought by Santa in his sleigh
St Nicholas is really his name and he has a big white beard
His sleigh is pulled by reindeers
Rudolph, leading the herd

Continue the tradition, put bright lights for all to see
Hang lots of holly around the room
And dress up the Christmas Tree
Cook mince pies and puddings, decorate the Christmas cake
Hurry and wrap up the presents
Today's Christmas for goodness sake

Martha Ann D'Souza

LOOKING FORWARD TO NEXT CHRISTMAS

Christmas Day is just one of those annual stepping stones
A frank barometer snapshot of life's ups and downs
Measured so slowly by laughter lines and frowns
While the fast-falling level in the sherry bottle
Reveals the hidden tensions and suppressed groans
Deciding which relative you'd most like to throttle!

Christmas Day is brim full of the happiness life brings.
As the years speed by and the traditions slowly grow.
Stockings are bulging, filled with insignificant things
And the children's faces shine with expectant glee
Joyous in the fun times that their Christmases show.
Do you remember that was once true for you and me?

But this Christmas Day looms large and is all the more blacker.
It has become the hardest time of a long, lonely year.
When families break, rent asunder like a novelty filled cracker
Loyalties are split and reluctant children shared between
While each guilty party suffers in silence and sheds a tear
Reflecting on what happened and what might have been.

What do future Christmases hold for those left behind?
Or those that set forth on the perilous path of independence?
Will the passing years heal all wounds, fill the gaps in your mind?
Will next Christmas be easier still? Will people get off their fence?
Will friends come out from the shadows and smile?
And welcome these now single people just once in a while?

Though Christmas past shouldn't be forgotten or untold
Knowing this year's Christmas present has been blackballed
In layers of false tinsel with curling bows knotted tight
Need not make us sad. Rather, stand tall and upright!
It's Christmases future that can hold us still, enthralled
Thinking of what promise - with another - they might hold.

Anne Rainbow

CHRISTMAS CATASTROPHE

Zawadi gnaws her little fingers, attempting
To satisfy the hunger gnawing at her distended belly.
She rubs her parched little face
Drying out in the blistering sun while
Her mother does her best to cradle
The body of bones on her sinking lap.

Barely two years old, yet unable to walk
Or leave the only security she knows,
The scrawny arms of a desperate woman awaiting
Release from the living death of an African war,
Of famine in the Congo and
Isolation from the rest of the world.

How can this be happening at the dawn
Of the twenty-first century?
Devastation and a rising death toll exceeding
Anything since the end of horrific world wars!
Millions already in the parched earth, millions to follow.
Food, water, medical relief, shelter,
The bare basics of survival lacking and unhurried.
The message of Christmas never to be heard.

No sex discrimination here as in Herod's slaughter of baby boys.
All children born to die, never to grow old,
But a sign to show nations that in spite of
Global wealth, ever-increasing knowledge and
New daily technology,
The most priceless gifts are not given,
Care, concern and compassionate hearts
For these innocent, suffering children!

Pat Heppel

INFORMATION

We hope you have enjoyed reading this book - and that you will continue to enjoy it in the coming years.

If you like reading and writing poetry drop us a line, or give us a call, and we'll send you a free information pack.

Alternatively if you would like to order further copies of this book or any of our other titles, then please give us a call or log onto our website at www.forwardpress.co.uk

**Anchor Books Information
Remus House
Coltsfoot Drive
Peterborough
PE2 9JX
(01733) 898102**

p.89 STAR
p.37 CHRISTMAS.